Cake Balls

Cake Balls

• • Zore Than 60 • •

DELECTABLE & WHIMSICAL
SWEET SPHERES OF GOODNESS

DEDE WILSON

THE HARVARD COMMON PRESS
BOSTON, MASSACHUSETTS

The Harvard Common Press
535 Albany Street
Boston, Massachusetts 02118
www.harvardcommonpress.com

Printed in China
Printed on acid-free paper

Food photography and prop styling by
Sabra Krock; props selected by Ed Gallagher;
food styling by Cynthia Groseclose

*Library of Congress Cataloging-in-
Publication Data*
Wilson, Dede.
  Cake balls: more than 60 delectable and
whimsical sweet spheres of goodness / Dede
Wilson.
    p. cm.
  Includes index.
  ISBN 978-1-55832-762-7 (hardback)
1. Cake. 2. Cooking, American. I. Title.
TX771.W469 2012
641.86'53--dc23
                                    2011039030

Special bulk-order discounts are available on
this and other Harvard Common Press books.
Companies and organizations may purchase
books for premiums or resale, or may arrange
a custom edition, by contacting the Marketing
Director at the address above.

10 9 8 7 6 5 4 3 2 1

To Juanita Plimpton & Mary McNamara

· MY LIFE MUSES ·

● ● ●

ACKNOWLEDGMENTS

Thank you to Maureen and Eric Lasher and the Harvard
Common Press team for knowing a great idea when they see it.

●

Thank you to Wilton Brands, Inc., for their fabulous
cake decorating and baking products.

●

Thank you to my enthusiastic tasters who offered helpful
critiques: David, Mary, Wally, Julie, Annie, Steve, Anne,
Juanita, Tom, Harry, Adrienne, Claudia, Dave, and my gym
ladies—Jennifer, Joan, Hannah, Caryn, and Christie.

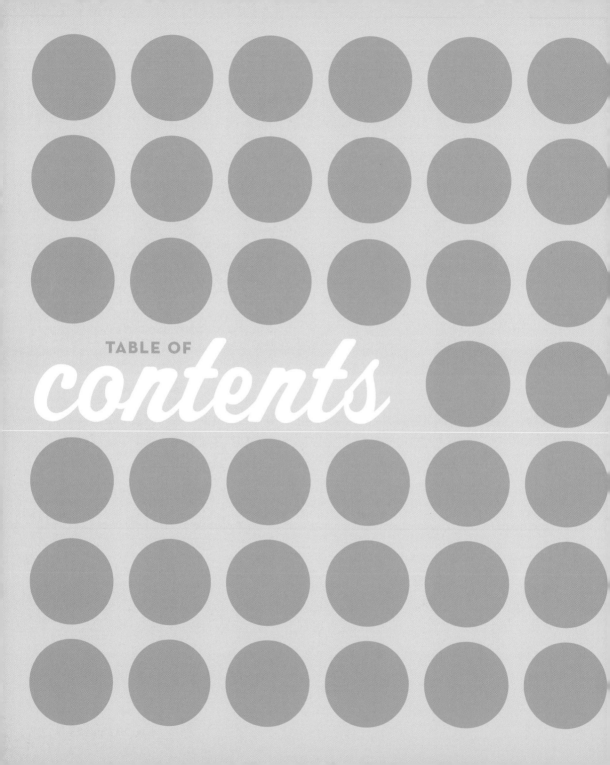

TABLE OF
contents

1

Baking & Creating Fabulous Cake Balls 12

2

The Basic Recipes 28

BASIC CAKE RECIPES

The Cake Balls 48

Cake Ball Creations 140

INTRODUCTION

What Is a Cake Ball?

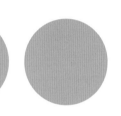

Maybe cake balls have already come into your life, just as cookies and cupcakes have. If not, get ready for fun and deliciousness! It is a rare occurrence for a "new" baked good to appear, and that is just one reason cake balls are so exciting. They are also easy and fun to make and eat and yet unique unto themselves.

Cake balls are, simply put, a combination of cake, a binder (like frosting), and a coating (usually chocolate). Perhaps you have seen versions on the Internet and elsewhere calling for boxed cake mixes and canned frosting (see page 32 for my take on this method). My approach to cake balls is taste-based, and in this book I guide you with from-scratch cake and frosting recipes, stressing high-quality ingredients. My cake balls look like a cross between a gussied-up doughnut hole and a large candy truffle. Their preparation can be as simple as using yellow buttermilk cake, vanilla frosting, and a coating of pure white chocolate, or they can be something quite elegant with deep, dark chocolate cake, fresh

raspberries, dark chocolate ganache binder, and a coating of bittersweet chocolate embellished with more berries. You will find both of those recipes in this book, as well as fun renditions like Confetti Cake Balls, Cappuccino Cake Balls, Zesty Lemon Cake Balls, and many others—more than 50 in all!

As with all of my books, my aim is to be your helper in the kitchen. I want you to have the most enjoyable and mouthwatering experience possible. I love hearing from readers; if you have any questions or want to share stories and pictures, please do not hesitate to contact me at dede@dedewilson.com.

HOW TO USE THIS BOOK

This book is set up to be as user-friendly as possible. Whether you want to make cake balls from scratch, try a cake mix, or create a cake ball with flavors of your own choosing, I have provided guidelines to ensure great results.

CHAPTER 1: BAKING AND CREATING FABULOUS CAKE BALLS provides you with the basics to begin making these tiny, tasty treats. Here you will find information on creating your own flavor combinations; a brief section on ingredients, equipment, and techniques; descriptions of purchased decorations that will greatly enhance your cake balls; and storage tips.

CHAPTER 2: THE BASIC RECIPES is where the fun begins; it is divided into two sections. The first part provides you with basic cake recipes, while the second has frostings, ganache, pastry cream, and other moist "binders" to combine with the cake "bases." All of these basic recipes are used in Chapter 3 in complete cake ball presentations, but you can also mix and match them as you please when devising your own flavor combos. Chapter 2 also contains a section on making cake balls using cake mixes and prepared frostings. When time is short, this is an option to consider, and I make suggestions for how to customize this approach to make the finished cake balls uniquely yours.

CHAPTER 3: THE CAKE BALLS is the heart of the book, where you will find more than 50 complete recipes for cake balls, including seasonal Red, White, and Blue Cake Balls; classics like Red Velvet; and soon-to-be favorites like Mocha Toffee Crunch, Boston Cream, and Confetti. Thinking outside the box, I also bring you Crème Brûlée Cake Balls and The Crunchie-Munchie, featuring potato chips, pretzels, and caramel popcorn.

CHAPTER 4: CAKE BALL CREATIONS brings you 10 recipes that show you how to use cake balls to make show-stopping desserts on a grand scale. How about a cone-shaped tower made of cake balls or a cake ball sundae party? These ideas and more are found in this chapter.

Last but not least, there is a **RESOURCES** section, which details purveyors that offer the ingredients and equipment you need for these recipes.

WHAT IS A CAKE BALL SERVING?

How many brownies or doughnut holes do you eat at one time? One? Three? I am sure it varies depending on the situation, your mood, and the richness of the dessert. Typically I find that people eat somewhere between two and four cake balls at a time. There are a few recipes in the book for which I suggest how many people the recipe will serve; however, most of the recipes give you the number of cake balls the recipe will yield, which I think you will find to be more helpful information.

Enjoy!

BAKING & CREATING

Fabulous Cake Balls

This chapter will help you understand the basics of making cake balls, from simple preparation techniques and suggested decorations to storage tips. I have also included a brief section on ingredients and equipment to help you make the best-tasting and best-looking cake balls possible.

CHOOSING YOUR CAKE BALL FLAVORS

As I mentioned in the Introduction, **Chapter 3: The Cake Balls** contains recipes that present entire flavor combinations. Baking, however, even within its limitations of exact measurements, is about exercising creativity. I find great joy in devising new ways to combine flavors and assume you do as well. **Chapter 2: The Basic Recipes** provides basic cake, frosting, and filling recipes so that you can create your own unique cake ball combinations.

For instance, for a fun kid's cake ball you could start with the basic White Cake recipe and fold a favorite candy or chocolate bar, finely chopped, into the batter. Combine this with vanilla Confectioners' Sugar Frosting and a dip in a chocolate coating in the child's favorite color. Alternatively, for a more adult cake ball you could use my Super-Easy Chocolate Cake recipe as your base, sprinkle the cake with Kahlúa, and combine it with Dark Chocolate Ganache. Dipped in bittersweet chocolate and dusted with gold powder, they will be sensational and very much like an individual truffle cake—elegant enough for a dinner party. Your imagination is the only limit in creating your own flavor combinations.

CAKE BALL BASICS

Before you make any of the cake balls in this book, please read this section and the sidebar "Cake Balls Without a Recipe" (pages 16 to 19) to familiarize yourself with the basic techniques of making cake balls. Every recipe is made up of a "base" (cake or brownie, for example), a "binder" (frosting, jam, lemon curd, and so forth) that holds the cake ball together, and a "coating" (melted chocolate, chopped nuts, or other) that covers the exterior of the cake ball. Here are the most important techniques for ensuring that your cake balls will be as good as can be.

Make sure your base is completely cool before proceeding. Crumble it into a bowl and use your fingers to create an evenly small crumb. (If you want to wear food-service gloves, be my guest.) A spoon or fork is just not as effective as your hands, although I have had good success with an old-fashioned pastry blender, particularly in the initial stages of crumbling the base. I also sometimes use a large, sturdy rubber or silicone spatula in a repetitive cutting motion. In the end, however, I use my hands to make sure the base is a mass of fine crumbs. With very moist bases, such as brownies, it's okay if you reduce the base to large moist clumps rather than crumbs.

Some bases are moist enough to hold together on their own (see Fudgy Brownies, page 37). The advantage here is that you are not adding any extra sweetness with a binder, but then again, nor do you have the opportunity to add additional flavor. You can first try and see whether a base will hold together on its own by rolling and compressing the crumbs in your hands. If it holds together in a firm ball, you are good to go without a binder. If you have an electric mixer with a flat paddle attachment, you can mix the dry crumbs until they begin to come together, then roll them into balls. However, if the base could be improved with the additional flavor and moisture provided by a binder, follow this procedure: Add a small amount of binder and combine with your base. You want just enough binder to help the base hold together and to add the flavor you want, so taste and assess texture as you go. While more binder might make the cake ball moister, it will also generally make it sweeter, so adjust as desired. Some recipes, such as the Boston Cream Cake Balls and the Zesty Lemon Cake Balls, need as much binder as possible to create the best flavor and texture. The important point to note is that the proportion is highly variable and up to your individual taste. Have fun experimenting. Take notes. If you make a cake ball and it is too moist and sweet, add less binder next time. Too dry? Make a note to add more binder to your next batch.

Use a food disher or ice cream scoop to help form the balls for the most even, professional-looking results. It will keep your yield in line, too! Have your base and binder combined and ready to go. I use a Zeroll #40 scoop (see Resources, page 166) to form golf ball–size balls. It is 1⁹⁄₁₆ inches in diameter and makes a great cookie dough scoop for large cookies as well.

To make smaller truffle-size balls, use the #100 scoop, which is 1³⁄₁₆ inches across. Dip the scoop into the mixture and fill up the scoop as you press and drag the it along the inside of the bowl, compressing the mixture against the bowl side as you drag. You want the bowl of the scoop to be slightly overfilled initially. Then drag the open edge of the scoop along the top edge of your bowl to level off the cake mixture. This will ensure that the scoop bowl is completely filled. Pop out the measured amount into your hand, and roll it between your palms into a firm, round ball. For the best-looking results, take your time at this point in the recipe to make sure that the ball is as round as possible. Place the balls on a baking sheet or tray as you form them.

If your cake ball is going to be dipped in a liquid coating such as chocolate or a confectioners' sugar glaze, refrigerate the balls before dipping. This will preserve the balls' round shape and make them easier to handle; you will also be less likely to leave crumbs in your liquid coating. Individual recipes provide specific instructions.

Have your chocolate or chocolate coating melted and fluid but not hot. Sugar glaze should be fluid and smooth. Place the liquid coating in a tall, narrow container; I often use a 2-cup liquid measuring cup. Drop one ball at a time in the coating and use two forks to help submerge the ball and toss it back and forth until it is completely coated. If you have a set of chocolate dipping tools, try using the loop-like tool or the two-pronged fork in one hand and a regular table fork in the other (this is what I do). You can also make a dipping tool with a plastic fork; simply break off and remove the inner tines, leaving the outer two. Remove the ball from the coating, perched on (but not pierced by) the loop or fork, and firmly tap the tool on the edge of the container, encouraging excess coating to flow back into the container. You want just enough coating clinging to the ball to cover it, or else excess will pool around the cake ball's base upon cooling and need to be trimmed away (see cutaway photos throughout the book to see

the desired coating thinness). Place the coated ball on a sheet pan lined with aluminum foil or parchment paper and continue with the remaining balls. If you are adding a dry decoration, such as chopped dried fruit, nuts, or sprinkles, apply them at this time, while the coating is still wet. Once all the balls are dipped, refrigerate them briefly to set the coating. Once set, you might find that the balls have developed a "foot," which is the technical term for the chocolate or liquid coating that has pooled around their base. Use a sharp paring knife to simply trim these extraneous pieces away, making the balls as neat and round as possible without cutting into the coating so deeply that you expose the cake inside. Place individual balls in fluted paper cups, if desired. Store in a single layer in an airtight container.

If you are going to skip the dipping step and simply coat your cake balls with a dry coating such as chopped nuts or cinnamon sugar (see page 25), then follow this technique for the best results: Do not refrigerate the balls once they are rolled. Pick up the balls one at a time and reroll them between your palms to warm and soften them, then immediately roll them in the dry coating. One technique that works very well is to have chopped nuts (for instance) on your work surface. Place the cake ball on top of the coating and roll it around in the coating, pressing the ball down into the coating as you roll. Place balls in fluted paper cups, if desired. Store in a single layer in an airtight container.

CUSTOMIZING CAKE BALLS TO YOUR TASTE

Almost every recipe has a base component (cake or brownie) and a binder component (frosting, ganache, jam, and so on). The amount of binder in each ingredient list will always be enough to complete your cake ball project. The amount I recommend to be combined with the base in the instructions will be a portion of the listed amount and is scaled to be just shy of what you will most likely actually need. This allows you to take a custom approach to your cake balls. Sometimes a cake is moister than it was the last time you baked it and the amount of binder needed is thus different from before, or perhaps you have a sweeter tooth than I do and want to add more binder. As long as the mixture holds together in a ball shape and is to your taste, it is the right amount!

*T*his sidebar might seem odd at first glance, existing alongside a collection of recipes, but hear me out. These recipes are tried and true and will get the job done when you want to follow instructions with a guaranteed result. Sometimes, however, we bakers want to stretch our creative muscles and branch out beyond formulas. Here are cake balls without a recipe, at a glance. Happy creating!

Start with your base, which is typically freshly baked cake but could also be leftover cake scraps, frozen pound cake (defrosted), purchased angel food or sponge cake, a mixture of cakes, or even coffee cake. It's your choice.

As an alternative, the base could be soft cookies, brownies, doughnuts, muffins, or unfrosted cupcakes. Chocolate or vanilla sandwich cookies work too, finely ground in a food processor.

Crumble the base in a large bowl using your hands or a pastry blender. You want an even crumb of your base mixture.

Now test your mixture; it might hold together without any binder at all. Compress the mixture firmly between your fingers and palms. If it holds a ball shape, you can proceed with a coating. If it is too crumbly—or you simply want to add additional flavor or moisture—

then a binder is called for. Binders can be anything from frosting to jam to lemon curd, honey, peanut butter, pastry cream, cream cheese, chocolate ganache, liqueur, or even liquid coffee creamer. You just need to add something a bit soft and sticky to the base to encourage it to hold together in a ball shape. If the base and binder taste good together and the texture works (that is, the mixture holds together in a ball), go for it. Always start with a small amount of binder; you can add more if needed.

Cake balls can be rolled into many sizes, but somewhere around golf ball–size gives the best base-to-binder-to-coating ratio for most mixtures. They can be a bit larger, but baseball size is too big; those will fall apart when eaten. On the other end of the spectrum, they can be as small as 1 inch across, and this size is great for very rich combinations. The idea is that they are a bite or two or three, no more. Use your hands, wearing food-service gloves or not, to roll into balls or, alternatively, use an ice cream scoop or food disher and finish them off with a roll between your palms (which is what I do).

Once rolled, refrigerate or freeze the cake balls at least long enough for them to firm up. Depending on a variety of factors (including choice of ingredients and temperature or texture of ingredients) this might be as brief as 30 minutes in the freezer or as long as 4 hours in the refrigerator. After they have firmed up, they can be frozen in airtight containers or zipper-top plastic bags until you're ready to finish them. If frozen, defrost before proceeding.

Along with a base and a binder, you need a coating to finish off the cake balls. Typically cake balls are dipped in melted chocolate (white, milk, or dark) or chocolate confectionery coating, but there are other options as well. Consider a confectioners' sugar glaze that hardens, which you can flavor with extracts, or even a dry coating such as a cinnamon-sugar mixture, finely chopped nuts, shaved chocolate, or shredded coconut. These dry coatings will work only with very moist cake balls, as they need something to stick to.

Last but not least, you can decorate your cake balls in a variety of ways. If they have been rolled in a dry coating, that's all they need. Cake balls dipped in chocolate or glaze can be left as is, or decorated further. While the chocolate or glaze is wet, you can sprinkle them with or roll them in chopped nuts, shredded coconut, shaved chocolate, sprinkles, nonpareils, or edible glitter, or you can affix a molded sugar decoration. After the chocolate sets, you can also use melted chocolate of the same or a different flavor or color in a parchment cone to decorate the cake balls with additional initials, zigzags, and so forth.

Once the cake balls are finished, consider placing each one in a miniature fluted paper cup. This will protect them and keep them looking their best for serving.

In general, cake balls are best refrigerated in single layers in airtight containers but served at room temperature. Use your best judgment and baking experience.

START WITH THE CAKE

CRUMBLE THE CAKE

ADD THE FROSTING

MIX BINDER WITH THE CAKE

TEST "HOLD TOGETHERNESS" OF MIXTURE

SCOOP AND FORM IT

LEVEL IT

MAKE IT ROUND

PREPARE TO DIP

DIP

DECORATE

ENJOY THE FINAL PRODUCT

Label Your Cake Ball

There is nothing wrong with dipping a cake ball in chocolate or chocolate coating and calling it a day. If you are like me, however, and like to know more about the flavors of the item you are about to pop into your mouth, you will appreciate the additional decorations that I suggest as the final flourishes. This will "label" the cake ball, as I take inspiration from the flavors within or from what the concept of the cake ball represents. For instance, crushed peppermint candy tops the Peppermint–White Chocolate Cake Balls, and I suggest a dusting of cocoa powder and ground cinnamon for the Cappuccino Cake Balls. By taking this little extra step, you are not only embellishing the cake balls a bit more but also helping the lucky eaters know what flavors await them.

INGREDIENTS, EQUIPMENT, AND TECHNIQUES

Here is a brief list of the most commonly used ingredients, equipment, and techniques in the recipes in this book.

Ingredients

FLOUR: I recommend King Arthur unbleached all-purpose flour. While I do suggest cake flour for fancy cakes in some of my other books, all-purpose flour works just fine for cake balls.

BAKING POWDER AND BAKING SODA: Make sure both are fresh, or else leavening power will be diminished. I use double-acting baking powder such as Davis or Rumford brands.

SALT: Use regular table salt, as other salts, such as kosher and coarse salts, will measure differently.

BUTTER: Recipes were tested with unsalted butter. I recommend Land O Lakes Unsalted Butter.

EGGS: Use brown or white Grade AA large eggs.

MILK, CREAM CHEESE, SOUR CREAM: Use full-fat varieties.

HEAVY CREAM: The recipes call for heavy cream; you may use cream labeled "heavy cream," "heavy whipping cream," or "whipping cream."

GRANULATED SUGAR: I recommend Domino granulated premium pure cane sugar.

LIGHT AND DARK BROWN SUGARS: These can be substituted for one another in the recipes. However, keep in mind that dark brown sugar will give you a very pronounced molasses flavor, which may or may not be desired. Pack brown sugar firmly into exact-size dry measuring cups.

CONFECTIONERS' SUGAR: I recommend Domino 10X confectioners' sugar.

EXTRACTS: Use pure vanilla and almond extracts. I like Nielsen-Massey.

CHOCOLATE: Most of the recipes were tested with Callebaut and Ghirardelli chocolates, as they are easily found in many supermarkets. Certain recipes use higher-end chocolates such as Scharffen Berger or Valrhona, and I

make specific recommendations in the ingredient lists; substituting with other chocolates will give different results and most likely not for the better. For white chocolate, I prefer the flavors of Callebaut and Valrhona. Do not try to melt chocolate morsels, which are formulated to hold their shape; they will melt eventually, but their melted texture will be thick and not suitable for dipping cake balls. While you can use melted Ghirardelli chocolate as a coating for your cake balls, it does not have as much cocoa butter as Callebaut, Scharffen Berger, or Valrhona and will therefore not be as fluid. Chocolate with a higher fluidity makes a more attractive, thinner outer coating for your cake balls, leaves less of a "foot," and as an added boon is easier to work with.

CHOCOLATE COATING: Also called confectionery coating, compound coating, and summer coating, these coatings come in white, milk, and dark chocolate flavors as well as every color of the rainbow (which often have a vanilla flavor). Brands I recommend are Merckens Compound Coating Chocolate and Wilton Candy Melts. You can also find coatings in flavors such as peanut butter, mint, orange, and strawberry. See Resources (page 164) for ordering information for all of these options.

COCOA POWDER: Recipes will specify natural or Dutch-processed cocoa powder, and they should not be substituted for one another. I use Hershey, Ghirardelli, and Scharffen Berger natural cocoa powder and Valrhona and Bensdorp Dutch-processed cocoa powder. The Blackout Cake Balls (page 57) use a specialty cocoa called Black Cocoa; it is different from those already mentioned and can be ordered from King Arthur Flour (see Resources, page 165). It has the dark color and rich flavor of the cocoa used in Oreo cookies.

NONSTICK COOKING SPRAY: Look for nonstick cooking spray in the oil aisle of the supermarket. I do not like the ones that have flour added; use spray made from simple unflavored oil, such as Pam.

FOOD COLORS: Depending on the recipe, I call for colored pastes, gels, liquids, or powders. The liquid type can be found in the baking aisle of the supermarket. The others can be found in craft or cake decorating stores or mail-ordered (see Resources, page 164).

Equipment

MEASURING CUPS AND SPOONS: High-quality measuring implements are a must. I use Cuisipro as well as those from King Arthur Flour, Sur La Table, and Williams-Sonoma. Believe it or not, a tablespoon can vary hugely in volume, as lesser brands are not calibrated to industry standards. Skip buying measuring tools at the dollar store, and certainly do not rely on those old dented ones from your grandmother.

ELECTRIC MIXER: Where required, these recipes were tested with a 5-quart KitchenAid stand mixer, which usually comes with three attachments. (One is a dough hook, which you won't need for these recipes.) The paddle attachment is used for creaming butter and sugar, while the balloon whip is used for whipping egg whites and cream. A handheld mixer can be used instead, but mixing times will be longer.

FOOD DISHERS: These look like (and can be used as) ice cream scoops. They make forming cake balls a breeze and yield a uniform size and shape every time. I use Zeroll brand #40 to make a perfect golf ball–size cake ball. The #100 is great for smaller truffle-size balls, such as for the Chocolate Chip Cookie Dough Cake Balls. To use, dip the scoop into a bowl of crumbled cake (with binder added, if using), overfilling the scoop and pressing along the side of the bowl as you go. Level it off against the top rim of the bowl, then pop the cake mixture out into your palms and roll into a ball.

FLUTED PAPER CUPS: These have many names: baking cups, muffin or cupcake liners, muffin or cupcake wrappers, and so on. They are usually slipped into muffin and cupcake tins before baking those treats. For this book I mostly use the mini size (meant for mini muffin or cupcake tins) to protect my finished golf ball–size cake balls. They come in a huge variety of colors and patterns and add flair to your desserts (see Resources, page 164).

Techniques

CRUMBLING YOUR CAKE BASE: The cakes in this book are baked in square and rectangular pans and need to be crumbled into a bowl after they cool. You can certainly use your fingers for the whole job (naked or in food-service gloves), but I find that an old-fashioned pastry blender also does a great job with the initial stage of crumbling. It cuts into the cake and breaks down the crumb very evenly. A spoon or fork is usually not effective enough. You can also try using the edge of a large, sturdy rubber or silicone spatula (not the broad side, which would mash the cake) in a repetitive cutting motion. Toward the end of the crumbling step, I always finish off with my hands to make sure the base is a mass of fine crumbs. (With very moist bases, such as brownies, the base can be reduced to large moist clumps rather than crumbs.)

MEASURING DRY INGREDIENTS: I transfer flour, confectioners' sugar, cocoa powder, and granulated sugar from their commercial packages into large airtight containers. To measure flour, whisk it first to aerate. For confectioners' sugar and cocoa powder, sift it first. For granulated sugar, you can measure right out of the container. For all of these dry items, use the exact-size dry measuring cup called for and dip it into the item so that the dry ingredient is mounded. Use the flat edge of a butter knife or icing spatula to sweep off the excess, using the top of the measuring cup as a guide. This is the "dip and sweep" method. Brown sugars should be firmly packed into exact-size measuring cups to the top and leveled off.

INGREDIENT TEMPERATURE: When a recipe suggests using room-temperature ingredients and you have forgotten to remove them from the refrigerator, there are a few tricks you can employ. For eggs, put them (still in the shell) in a bowl of warm water for 5 minutes. Room-temperature eggs will incorporate more readily into butter and sugar during the creaming phase. If you need to soften butter, familiarity with your microwave will be very helpful. I take butter straight from the refrigerator and go with 10-second bursts on high power. Foil wrappers cannot go in the microwave, only paper wrappers, so unwrap and place on a plate if necessary. You are aiming to soften, not melt, so take care. Alternatively, you can grate cold butter on the largest holes of a box grater; the small pieces will warm up very quickly. Cream cheese blends much more readily when used at room temperature as well. You can remove it from its foil wrapper and soften it in the microwave using the same technique as for butter.

*U*pon melting, your chocolate or coating might be very thick—too thick to coat your cake balls. There are reasons and solutions. First of all, shop wisely. I tested these recipes with fresh Callebaut, Ghirardelli, Scharffen Berger, and Valrhona chocolates. With any chocolate, make sure it has been stored correctly—wrapped airtight in a dry, cool location, preferably for less than 6 months. Do not try to melt chocolate morsels or chips; they are formulated to hold their shape.

If you are using real chocolate (which has cocoa butter as its fat) and experiencing difficulty melting it smoothly, you can try adding cocoa butter to your mixture to thin it out (see Resources, page 164). You could also look for couverture chocolate, which has a naturally high cocoa butter content and melts easily to a fluid consistency. Couverture chocolate, which can be dark, milk, or white, is a specialty product that you will most likely have to mail-order or purchase from a specialty store (see Resources, page 164). Couverture chocolate has at least 32 percent cocoa butter. The percentage is sometimes listed, or you can ask the supplier if the chocolate is a couverture. Do not confuse the cocoa butter percentage with the cacao mass percentage, which is very commonly listed on packages these days. For example, if the package says "semisweet chocolate 50%" it is referring to the cacao mass, not the cocoa butter.

Always melt chocolate over low heat. For dark chocolates, you can try the microwave on low power (if you are very familiar with your microwave), but for milk and white chocolates I suggest using a double boiler with barely simmering water in the bottom. Overheating will burn chocolate and yield a thick, gloppy mess. Any moisture at all (such as a drop of water from a newly washed bowl) will cause chocolate to seize upon melting.

Chocolate coatings, with their vegetable oil (non–cocoa butter) content, should also be wrapped airtight and stored in a cool, dry place. If coatings have been stored for too long or are overheated, they will be thick upon melting. There are date codes on most coating bags or wrappers. Make sure that the coatings are less than 9 months old and that you melt them on very low power in the microwave or over barely simmering water in a double boiler. (Note that manufacturers often claim that their coatings have an 18-month shelf life. For melting purposes, I disagree.) If they are still thick upon melting, you can try stirring in a bit of vegetable shortening, unsalted butter, or flavorless vegetable oil (in that order of preference). If you will be making a lot of cake balls and using coatings, you might want to purchase Paramount Crystals, which is a specialty product (see Resources, page 165) made of partially hydrogenated palm kernel oil. It is inexpensive and specifically made to thin out coatings.

MAKING A PARCHMENT CONE

Parchment cones are perfect for making designs on top of finished cake balls with melted chocolate or chocolate coatings. Cut a triangle out of parchment paper with one longer side (shorter sides should be about 8 inches and the longer side about 12 inches). These directions are for right-handed folks; reverse for lefties. Hold the center of the long side with your left thumb and index finger. Using your right hand, take the top corner and roll it toward you. The cone will begin to form. Align that top tip with the corner on the right. Let go with your left hand and now hold these two right-side corners together with your right hand. Repeat with the bottom corner, rolling it up and aligning it with the right-hand corner (using your left hand). Now use both hands to jiggle the aligned corners back and forth so that the point of the cone tightens, then fold down the open side a few times to seal the cone shape into place. The cone is ready to fill. Do not fill it more than halfway. Fold the open side closed, then use scissors to snip a very small hole from the tip; you can always make the hole larger, if needed.

APPLYING DRY COATINGS

Some cake balls are very moist, such as those moistened with pastry cream, cream cheese frosting, lemon curd, or jams, and these cake balls can be coated with a dry coating such as chopped nuts, shredded coconut, or shaved chocolate. There are some techniques to employ to coat cake balls with dry coatings successfully. First of all, as mentioned, start with a moist cake ball.

If you are using something dry and powdery, like confectioners' sugar or cocoa powder, sift it. If you are using something dry and granular, like cinnamon sugar, make sure there are no lumps. Place the coating in a small bowl, drop the cake balls into the bowl one at a time, and toss the ball around until coated.

Nuts should be chopped very finely. Sweetened long-shred coconut should be chopped a bit so that it more evenly covers the cake ball. To shave chocolate, start with a block of chocolate. Use a large chef's knife to shave shards off of the chocolate; you are aiming at creating small, fine shavings. For nuts, coconut, and chocolate shavings, proceed as follows: Spread a small amount of the dry coating on a flat surface, such as a cutting board. Place a cake ball on top of the dry ingredients and use your palm to roll the ball around, using a firm downward pressure as you roll. Keep rolling until the ball is completely covered with the dry coating. Repeat with the remaining balls; keep adding dry coating to the work surface as needed. Cake balls with dry coatings typically have a shorter shelf life than those dipped in chocolate or chocolate coating because they are not sealed airtight by the chocolate.

CAKE BALL DECORATIONS

The recipes in this book range from very easy with simple chocolate coatings to fancier versions such as those painted with edible gold powder, sprinkled with nonpareils, or adorned with a molded sugar carrot. When envisioning your own cake ball designs, take into account the plethora of decorations available.

NONPAREILS: These are tiny sugar balls, classically available in white but these days found in all the colors of the rainbow. They also come in various sizes.

COLORED SUGAR: Available in fine and coarse textures, these not only come in all colors but also come in color blends, such as red, white, and blue or pastel mixtures.

COLORED POWDERS: These come in every color of the rainbow and can be used wet or dry. There are also silver and gold powders that look quite metallic yet are edible.

EDIBLE GLITTER: This is actual edible sparkly glitter that comes in all colors.

SPRINKLE DECORATIONS: This is what I call the very large array of decorations that can be simply sprinkled on your baked goods, from chocolate or rainbow sprinkles (sometimes called jimmies) to those shaped like tiny autumn leaves, flowers, hearts, and butterflies, or even pigs, dog bones, dinosaurs, and cows. What they have in common is that they are all very small and easy to use—just sprinkle them onto a cake ball that has just been dipped, while the chocolate coating is still wet.

MOLDED SUGAR DECORATIONS: This might just be the largest category of them all. For these recipes I focus on smaller molded decorations, ones that would look proportionately correct on top of a finished cake ball. You can find everything from carrots to crosses, tiny dog faces to bees, baby booties, princess crowns, gardening tools, seashells, and race cars. Placing one of these on a cake ball might be the easiest way to customize your creation. See Resources (page 164).

STORING CAKE BALLS

Some cake balls, such as the crème brûlée balls, have very specific storage instructions. Always follow the storage information in the individual recipe. In general, however, most of these cake balls are best if refrigerated for storage but then served at room temperature.

For longer storage, many of the cake balls can be frozen; this is best done once they are formed into balls but before they are coated with wet or dry coatings. After forming balls, chill well to firm up, then place in airtight containers and freeze. Specific instructions are given in individual recipes.

Consider placing your finished cake balls in fluted paper cups; these will protect the outer coatings—and make for a more attractive presentation. Store your cake balls in a single layer in airtight containers whether they are stored at room temperature, refrigerated, or frozen.

2

The Basic Recipes

The recipes in this chapter are used throughout the book, but I hope that you will also use them as basics from which to craft your own cake ball creations. Choose a cake, choose a frosting or filling, and go wild!

Note that these recipes were developed specifically with cake balls in mind. For instance, the brownie recipe is not my favorite to eat as a bar as you would a traditional brownie. The texture was developed specifically to hold together by itself when rolled into a ball.

Yellow Buttermilk Cake

This is a buttery yellow cake, perfect for cake balls that need a fairly neutral flavor background. It works well combined with everything from jam to liqueur to ganache and various frostings.

● ● ●

1 Position a rack in the middle of the oven. Preheat the oven to 350°F. Coat the inside of a 9 x 13-inch rectangular pan with nonstick cooking spray; set aside.

2 Whisk together the flour, baking powder, and salt in a medium bowl to aerate and combine; set aside.

3 In a large bowl with an electric mixer on medium-high speed, beat the butter until creamy, about 2 minutes. Add the sugar gradually and beat until very light and fluffy, about 3 minutes, scraping down the bowl once or twice. Beat in the vanilla.

4 Beat in the eggs one at a time, scraping down after each addition and allowing each egg to be absorbed before continuing. Add the flour mixture in four additions, alternating with the buttermilk. Begin and end with the flour mixture and beat briefly until smooth. Pour the batter into the prepared pan.

5 Bake for about 30 minutes, or until a toothpick inserted in the center shows a few moist crumbs when removed. Let cool completely in the pan on a wire rack. The cake is ready to use. Alternatively, double-wrap the pan in plastic wrap and store at room temperature for up to 1 day before proceeding.

Variations: This yellow cake works with every frosting in the book as well as numerous binders such as jams, lemon curd, and pastry cream. It is the perfect cake to experiment with when designing your own cake balls. How about yellow cake, a bit of Kahlúa, espresso buttercream, and a dip in dark chocolate; or yellow cake, apricot jam, and a dip in white chocolate?

MAKES ONE 9 X 13-INCH BASE CAKE *(about 12 cups crumbs)*

2½ cups all-purpose flour

1 tablespoon baking powder

½ teaspoon salt

1 cup (2 sticks) unsalted butter, at room temperature, cut into pieces

2 cups sugar

1 tablespoon pure vanilla extract

5 large eggs, at room temperature

1¼ cups low-fat buttermilk

Yellow Cake

This is a buttery-tasting yellow cake that uses melted butter, making it a very simple batter to prepare with just a whisk. Use this recipe when time is of the essence.

MAKES ONE 9 X 13-INCH BASE CAKE (about 12 cups crumbs)

2¾ cups all-purpose flour

1 cup sugar

1 tablespoon baking powder

¼ teaspoon salt

4 large eggs, at room temperature

1 cup whole milk, at room temperature

1 cup (2 sticks) unsalted butter, melted and cooled to lukewarm

1 teaspoon pure vanilla extract

1   Position a rack in the middle of the oven. Preheat the oven to 350°F. Coat the inside of a 9 x 13-inch rectangular pan with nonstick cooking spray; set aside.

2   Whisk together the flour, sugar, baking powder, and salt in a large bowl to aerate and combine; set aside.

3   Whisk the eggs and milk together in a medium bowl until thoroughly combined. Whisk in the melted butter and vanilla.

4   Pour the wet ingredients over the dry ingredients and whisk until combined. Pour the batter into the prepared pan.

5   Bake for about 25 minutes, or until a toothpick inserted in the center shows a few moist crumbs when removed. The cake might just begin to brown along the edges. Let cool completely in the pan on a wire rack. The cake is ready to use. Alternatively, double-wrap the pan in plastic wrap and store at room temperature for up to 1 day before proceeding.

SUPER-EASY
Chocolate Cake

Need a chocolate cake in a hurry? No mixer is required—just two bowls, a whisk, and a rubber spatula. This cake contains no eggs or dairy, making it vegan as well. Sift the cocoa powder before measuring to remove any lumps.

1   Position a rack in the middle of the oven. Preheat the oven to 350°F. Coat the inside of a 9 x 13-inch rectangular pan with nonstick cooking spray; set aside.

2   Whisk together the flour, sugar, cocoa, baking soda, and salt in a large bowl to aerate and combine; set aside.

3   Whisk together the water, oil, vinegar, and vanilla in a medium bowl.

4   Pour the wet ingredients over the dry ingredients and whisk vigorously until combined and smooth. Pour the batter into the prepared pan.

5   Bake for about 25 minutes, or until a toothpick inserted in the center shows a few moist crumbs when removed. Let cool completely in the pan on a wire rack. The cake is ready to use. Alternatively, double-wrap the pan in plastic wrap and store at room temperature for up to 1 day before proceeding.

Note: **For ease of preparation, I make this in my stand mixer, but you can get perfectly fine results if you whisk briskly by hand.**

MAKES ONE 9 X 13-INCH BASE CAKE *(about 13 cups crumbs)*

3 cups all-purpose flour

2 cups sugar

2/3 cup sifted natural cocoa powder

2 teaspoons baking soda

1 teaspoon salt

2 cups room-temperature water

2/3 cup flavorless vegetable oil, such as canola or sunflower

2 tablespoons apple cider vinegar or distilled white vinegar

1 tablespoon pure vanilla extract

Straight from the Box

By their very definition cake balls are a casual, fun confection. If I am making chocolate truffles I am going to pull out all the stops with the most premium of ingredients, but cake balls can and should be a fun baking project for bake sales, kids' parties, and the like, and sometimes you want a quick and easy solution. This is where commercial products like cake mixes and prepared frostings can help. Truth be told, before writing this book I had very little experience using a boxed cake mix. In the interest of seeing how they might help you get the job done quickly, I dove in and found that for cake balls, they work well. You will not have that homemade taste or as much control over the quality of ingredients, but it is a valid option. Here's the lowdown, if you want to take this approach.

MAKES ABOUT 3 DOZEN GOLF BALL–SIZE CAKE BALLS

1 (18.25-ounce) package cake mix
1 (16-ounce) container prepared frosting
18 ounces chocolate coating

1   Prepare the cake according to the directions on the package, baking it in a 9 x 13-inch pan. Let cool completely.

2   Crumble the cake into a large bowl. Add about half a can of frosting and mix it in thoroughly. Add only enough frosting so that the cake holds together when rolled into a ball. You can determine the correct amount by the texture. Roll the mixture into golf ball–size cake balls. Place in large, flat, airtight containers or on pie plates covered with plastic wrap (that's what I do). Refrigerate for 1 to 2 hours or freeze for 30 minutes, until very firm.

3   Line two rimmed baking sheets with parchment paper or aluminum foil. Melt the chocolate coating in the microwave or in the top of a double boiler set over barely simmering water. Dip the balls one at a time and place, evenly spaced, on the prepared pans. Refrigerate briefly, until the chocolate is set. Place each cake ball in a fluted paper cup, if desired. Place in a single layer in an airtight container and refrigerate for up to 4 days. Bring to room temperature before serving.

Variations: **It's as easy as choosing another flavor cake, frosting, and coating. Try banana cake with chocolate frosting and white chocolate coating; white cake with milk chocolate frosting and dark chocolate coating; confetti cake with confetti frosting and white chocolate coating; and so on—it's your choice. You can further customize your cake mixes by adding chopped nuts, flaked coconut, or chopped dried fruit to the cake batter before baking.**

Red Velvet Cake

Many people mistakenly think that red velvet cake is a chocolate cake. It actually has very little cocoa in the batter; my version has more than most. It does have a reddish, chocolaty color, due to the small amount of cocoa powder and a large quantity of red food coloring. Many recipes suggest doubling the amount of red food coloring; feel free to adjust as you like. I have listed this cake in the Basics section because it is used more than once in Chapter 3, and I bet you will find multiple uses for it too.

1 Position a rack in the middle of the oven. Preheat the oven to 350°F. Coat the inside of a 9 x 13-inch rectangular pan with nonstick cooking spray; set aside.

2 Whisk together the flour, cocoa, baking soda, and salt in a medium bowl to aerate and combine; set aside.

3 In a separate bowl, whisk together the buttermilk and vinegar; set aside.

4 In a large bowl with an electric mixer on medium-high speed, beat the butter until creamy, about 2 minutes. Add the sugar gradually and beat until very light and fluffy, about 3 minutes, scraping down the bowl once or twice. Beat in the vanilla and red food coloring until thoroughly combined.

5 Beat in the eggs one at a time, scraping down after each addition and allowing each egg to be absorbed before continuing. Add the flour mixture in four additions, alternating with the buttermilk mixture. Begin and end with the flour mixture and beat briefly until smooth. Pour the batter into the prepared pan.

6 Bake for about 25 minutes, or until a toothpick inserted in the center shows a few moist crumbs when removed. The cake will have begun to come away from the sides of the pan. Let cool completely in the pan on a wire rack. The cake is ready to use. Alternatively, double-wrap the pan in plastic wrap and store at room temperature for up to 1 day before proceeding.

MAKES ONE 9 X 13-INCH BASE CAKE (*about 9½ cups crumbs*)

- 1¾ cups all-purpose flour
- 2 tablespoons plus 1 teaspoon sifted natural cocoa powder
- 1 teaspoon baking soda
- ½ teaspoon salt
- 1 cup low-fat buttermilk, at room temperature
- 1 teaspoon apple cider vinegar or distilled white vinegar
- ½ cup (1 stick) unsalted butter, at room temperature, cut into pieces
- 1½ cups sugar
- 1 teaspoon pure vanilla extract
- 1 tablespoon red liquid or gel food coloring
- 2 large eggs, at room temperature

White Cake

Lighter in texture, paler in color, and subtler in flavor than yellow cake, white cake is perfect when combined with delicate flavors such as Pastry Cream (page 46) and White Chocolate Ganache (page 43). A golden brown, thin, somewhat crispy edge might develop during baking, which is hard to crumble. Feel free to cut it away before crumbling the cooled cake.

MAKES ONE 9 X 13-INCH BASE CAKE *(about 10 cups crumbs)*

2 cups all-purpose flour

1 tablespoon baking powder

½ teaspoon salt

4 large egg whites, at room temperature

1½ cups whole milk, at room temperature

½ cup (1 stick) unsalted butter, at room temperature, cut into small pieces

1½ cups sugar

2 teaspoons pure vanilla extract

1   Position a rack in the middle of the oven. Preheat the oven to 350°F. Coat the inside of a 9 x 13-inch rectangular pan with nonstick cooking spray; set aside.

2   Whisk together the flour, baking powder, and salt in a medium bowl to aerate and combine; set aside.

3   Whisk together the egg whites and milk in a small bowl; set aside.

4   In a large bowl with an electric mixer on medium-high speed, beat the butter until creamy, about 2 minutes. Add the sugar gradually and beat until very light and fluffy, about 3 minutes, scraping down the bowl once or twice. Beat in the vanilla.

5   Add the flour mixture in three additions, alternating with the egg white mixture. Begin and end with the flour mixture and beat briefly until smooth. Pour the batter into the prepared pan.

6   Bake for about 30 minutes, or until a toothpick inserted in the center shows a few moist crumbs when removed. The cake might just begin to brown along the edges. Let cool completely in the pan on a wire rack. The cake is ready to use. Alternatively, double-wrap the pan in plastic wrap and store at room temperature for up to 1 day before proceeding.

Carrot Cake

At first glance you might not think of carrot cake as versatile, but beyond combining it with cream cheese frosting, it works well with lemon curd, pastry cream, or any basic vanilla frosting. This cake is also moist enough to hold its ball shape without any binder whatsoever, if you compress it enough.

1 Position a rack in the middle of the oven. Preheat the oven to 350°F. Coat the inside of a 9 x 13-inch rectangular pan with nonstick cooking spray; set aside.

2 Whisk together the flour, baking powder, cinnamon, baking soda, and salt in a medium bowl to aerate and combine. Toss in the nuts and raisins until they are coated.

3 Whisk together the oil and brown sugar in a large bowl until smooth. Whisk in the eggs one at a time, allowing each one to be absorbed before continuing, then whisk in the vanilla. Fold in the carrots. Fold in the dry mixture until just combined using a large rubber spatula. Pour the batter into the prepared pan.

4 Bake for about 40 minutes, or until a toothpick inserted in the center shows a few moist crumbs when removed. Let cool completely in the pan on a wire rack. The cake is ready to use. Alternatively, double-wrap the pan in plastic wrap and store at room temperature for up to 1 day before proceeding.

MAKES ONE 9 X 13-INCH BASE CAKE (*about 13 cups crumbs*)

2 cups all-purpose flour

2 teaspoons baking powder

2 teaspoons ground cinnamon

1 teaspoon baking soda

1 teaspoon salt

1¼ cups toasted chopped walnuts or pecans

1¼ cups dark raisins

1¼ cups vegetable oil

2 cups firmly packed light brown sugar

4 large eggs, at room temperature

2 teaspoons pure vanilla extract

4 cups lightly packed finely grated carrots (about 1 pound)

Banana Cake

This is a very flavorful, rich, moist banana cake that lends itself to variations: Add chocolate chips, other nuts, raisins, or other dried fruit for a new take on this classic. Make sure to use very ripe bananas—they should show absolutely no green and have some black spots. Do not puree the bananas; rather, slice them into a measuring cup and mash down a bit with a fork to measure.

MAKES ONE 9 x 13-INCH BASE CAKE *(about 10²/₃ cups crumbs)*

2 cups all-purpose flour

1 teaspoon baking soda

½ teaspoon salt

½ cup walnut halves, toasted and finely chopped

½ cup (1 stick) unsalted butter, at room temperature, cut into pieces

¾ cup firmly packed brown sugar

½ cup granulated sugar

1 teaspoon pure vanilla extract

2 large eggs, at room temperature

1 cup coarsely mashed ripe bananas (about 2 large)

½ cup low-fat buttermilk or sour cream

1   Position a rack in the middle of the oven. Preheat the oven to 350°F. Coat the inside of a 9 x 13-inch rectangular pan with nonstick cooking spray; set aside.

2   Whisk together the flour, baking soda, and salt in a medium bowl to aerate and combine. Toss in the nuts until they are coated; set aside.

3   In a large bowl with an electric mixer on medium-high speed, beat the butter until creamy, about 2 minutes. Add the sugars gradually and beat until very light and fluffy, about 3 minutes. Scrape down the bowl once or twice and then beat in the vanilla.

4   Beat in the eggs one at a time, scraping down after each addition and allowing each egg to be absorbed before continuing. Beat in the bananas. Add the flour mixture in four additions, alternating with the buttermilk. Begin and end with the flour mixture and beat briefly until smooth. Pour the batter into the prepared pan.

5   Bake for about 30 minutes, or until a toothpick inserted in the center shows a few moist crumbs when removed. The cake will be a light golden brown overall. Let cool completely in the pan on a wire rack. The cake is ready to use. Alternatively, double-wrap the pan in plastic wrap and store at room temperature for up to 1 day before proceeding.

Fudgy Brownies

When rolled into little rounds for cake balls, brownies take on a whole new dimension. Use this recipe when you want a dense, fudgy cake ball. There is nothing light and subtle about this base recipe. As with traditional brownies, nuts are optional, but I think they add texture and cut the sweetness in a positive way.

1 Position a rack in the middle of the oven. Preheat the oven to 350°F. Coat the inside of an 8-inch square pan with nonstick cooking spray; set aside.

2 Melt the butter in a medium saucepan on top of the stove or in a medium bowl in the microwave. Remove from the heat. Whisk in the sugar, cocoa, vanilla, and salt until combined. Allow to cool for a minute or two, so as not to cook the eggs. Whisk in the eggs one at a time, allowing each egg to be absorbed before continuing. Add the flour and nuts, if using, and fold in by hand just until combined. Pour the batter into the prepared pan.

3 Bake for about 15 minutes, or until a toothpick inserted in the center shows many moist crumbs. Do not overbake. Let cool in the pan completely on a wire rack. The brownies are ready to use. Alternatively, double-wrap the pan in plastic wrap and store at room temperature for up to 1 day before proceeding.

Note: **With brownies it is hard to gauge doneness—they will seem wet in the center compared to the other cakes in the book, but they are done! Do not overbake or they will lose their inherent fudginess. Also, please note that this brownie is meant to be turned into a cake ball. It is extra sticky and moist. I do not use this recipe when I want a brownie for eating in the traditional manner, where more nuanced textures are desired.**

MAKES ONE 8-INCH SQUARE BASE BROWNIE *(about 4½ cups crumbs)*

½ cup (1 stick) unsalted butter, cut into pieces

1 cup sugar

¾ cup sifted natural cocoa powder

1 teaspoon pure vanilla extract

¼ teaspoon salt

2 large eggs, at room temperature

⅔ cup toasted chopped nuts, such as walnuts or pecans (optional)

½ cup all-purpose flour

Milk Chocolate Brownies

Milk chocolate lovers, I have created a milk chocolate brownie just for you! Combine this with milk chocolate ganache for a milk chocolate–laden cake ball. The key is that you must use a high cacao mass milk chocolate, such as Valrhona Jivara (40 percent) or Scharffen Berger Milk Chocolate (41 percent). Using a high cacao percentage milk chocolate yields a moist, luscious milk chocolate brownie. This is one time when I strongly recommend not making any chocolate substitutions.

●　●　●

MAKES ONE 8-INCH SQUARE BASE BROWNIE *(about 5 cups crumbs)*

1 cup all-purpose flour

Pinch of salt

5 ounces milk chocolate, such as Valrhona Jivara, Scharffen Berger Milk Chocolate, or other high cacao mass (40% or above) milk chocolate

½ cup (1 stick) unsalted butter, at room temperature, cut into tablespoon-size pieces

⅔ cup sugar

2 large eggs, at room temperature

1 teaspoon pure vanilla extract

1　Position a rack in middle of the oven. Preheat the oven to 350°F. Coat an 8-inch square pan with nonstick cooking spray; set aside.

2　Whisk the flour and salt together in a small bowl to aerate and combine; set aside.

3　Melt the milk chocolate and butter together in the top of a double boiler over barely simmering water or in the microwave. Stir until smooth and let cool slightly.

4　In a large bowl with an electric mixer on medium-high speed, beat the sugar, eggs, and vanilla until light and fluffy, about 3 minutes. Gently fold in the chocolate-butter mixture until a few chocolate streaks remain. Fold the flour mixture into the batter until just combined. Spread evenly into the prepared pan.

5　Bake for about 18 minutes, or until a toothpick inserted in the center shows many moist crumbs. The brownies do not really change color. Do not overbake. Let cool completely in the pan on a wire rack. The brownies are ready to use. Alternatively, double-wrap the pan in plastic wrap and store at room temperature for up to 1 day before proceeding.

Confectioners' Sugar Frosting

This is a very easy frosting and probably the kind you loved when you were a child. It is the most commonly used in home baking and has that nostalgia factor. Confectioners' sugar–based frostings require a bit of leeway. If the frosting is too thin, add a bit more confectioners' sugar; if too thick, add a little milk. The key to making this silky smooth and creamy is to beat it for a long time, until it's ultrasmooth. This recipe halves easily for those recipes where a half batch is called for.

In a large bowl with an electric mixer on medium-high speed, beat the butter until creamy, about 2 minutes. Gradually add ½ cup of the confectioners' sugar, beating until light and fluffy, about 3 minutes, scraping down the bowl once or twice. Add the remaining 4½ cups confectioners' sugar, the milk, and the vanilla, and beat on high speed until silky smooth. The frosting is ready to use. It is best if used immediately, but it may be refrigerated in an airtight container for up to 4 days. (Bring to room temperature and rebeat before using.)

MAKES ABOUT 2½ CUPS

9 tablespoons (1 stick plus 1 tablespoon) unsalted butter, at room temperature, cut into small pieces

5 cups sifted confectioners' sugar, plus extra as needed

4½ tablespoons whole milk, plus extra as needed

1¼ teaspoons pure vanilla extract

Cream Cheese Frosting

Here is a classic cream cheese frosting for carrot cake balls or any other cake balls where you might like its tangy, sweet flavor. This makes a generous amount, as far as cake ball creation is concerned. You can easily halve the recipe when a half batch is called for.

● ● ●

MAKES 1¾ CUPS

8 ounces full-fat cream cheese or Neufchâtel cheese, at room temperature, cut into pieces

3 tablespoons unsalted butter, at room temperature, cut into pieces

1⅓ cups sifted confectioners' sugar

In a large bowl with an electric mixer on medium-high speed, beat the cream cheese until smooth, about 2 minutes; you want to eliminate any lumps. Add the butter and beat on medium-high speed until very smooth, scraping down the bowl once or twice. Add half of the sugar, beating on low speed until incorporated, then beat in the remaining sugar and beat until smooth and creamy. The frosting is ready to use. It is best if used immediately, but it may be refrigerated in an airtight container for up to 4 days. (Bring to room temperature and rebeat before using.)

Fudgy Chocolate Frosting

This recipe is not based on actual fudge, but it is loaded with chocolaty, fudgy flavor. Like all confectioners' sugar–based frostings, the texture can be adjusted by adding more confectioners' sugar for a thicker texture or more milk to thin it out.

● ● ●

In a large bowl with an electric mixer on medium-high speed, beat the butter until creamy, about 2 minutes. Gradually add ½ cup of the sugar, beating until beginning to combine, about 2 minutes, scraping down the bowl once or twice. Add the remaining 1½ cups sugar, the melted chocolate, vanilla, and milk, and beat on high speed until completely smooth and creamy. The frosting is ready to use. It is best if used immediately, but it may be refrigerated in an airtight container for up to 4 days. (Bring to room temperature and rebeat before using.)

MAKES ABOUT 1½ CUPS

- **4 tablespoons (½ stick) unsalted butter, at room temperature, cut into pieces**
- **2 cups sifted confectioners' sugar, plus extra as needed**
- **2½ ounces unsweetened chocolate, melted and slightly cooled**
- **½ teaspoon pure vanilla extract**
- **⅓ cup whole milk, plus extra as needed**

Dark Chocolate Ganache

This ganache is the darkest, richest chocolate icing in the book. The chocolate that you use will greatly affect the result in terms of flavor and texture. Given the balance of ingredients suggested in this recipe, using chocolate with a cacao mass content higher than 55 percent will often cause the ganache to "break" and not come together. If this happens, just whisk in some extra chilled cream or buzz it with an immersion blender and it should come together (but it would be better to use the recommended chocolates). You can easily halve this recipe when a half batch of ganache is called for.

MAKES ABOUT 2½ CUPS

1½ cups heavy cream

12 ounces semisweet chocolate, finely chopped, such as Valrhona Equatoriale or Callebaut

1 Place the cream in a large saucepan and bring to a boil over medium heat.

2 Remove from the heat and immediately sprinkle the chocolate into the cream. Cover and allow to sit for 5 minutes. The heat of the cream should melt the chocolate. Gently stir the ganache until smooth. If the chocolate is not melting, place the pan over very low heat, stirring often, until melted, taking care not to burn the chocolate. Let cool at room temperature until spreadable. The ganache is ready to use. (You may hasten the chilling process by stirring the pan over an ice bath. If it becomes too firm, or if you would like to return it to a softer state, simply place over hot water or microwave briefly.) The ganache may be refrigerated for up to 1 week or frozen for up to 1 month in an airtight container.

Milk Chocolate Ganache

Following the basic ganache premise of combining chocolate and cream, this is a milk chocolate ganache that works beautifully with the Milk Chocolate Brownies and the Super-Easy Chocolate Cake, but feel free to combine it with other cakes and bases as well. This recipe both halves and doubles perfectly.

1   Place the cream in a large saucepan and bring to a boil over medium heat.

2   Remove from the heat and immediately sprinkle the chocolate into the cream. Cover and allow to sit for 5 minutes. The heat of the cream should melt the chocolate. Gently stir the ganache until smooth. If the chocolate is not melting, place over very low heat, stirring often, until melted, taking care not to burn the chocolate. Let cool at room temperature until spreadable. The ganache is ready to use. (You may hasten the chilling process by stirring the pan over an ice bath. If it becomes too firm, or if you would like to return it to a softer state, simply place over hot water or microwave briefly.) The ganache may be refrigerated for up to 1 week or frozen for up to 1 month in an airtight container.

MAKES ABOUT 2½ CUPS

1½ cups heavy cream

1 pound milk chocolate, finely chopped, such as Callebaut, Valrhona Jivara, or Scharffen Berger

White Chocolate Ganache

If you want the most pronounced chocolate flavor possible when using white chocolate, make sure it has cocoa butter listed as its fat and not palm or cottonseed oil or other fats. This works wonderfully with yellow and white cakes in particular.

To make White Chocolate Ganache, follow the directions for Milk Chocolate Ganache, above. For best results, use a high-quality white chocolate, such as Callebaut or Valrhona Ivoire.

MAKES ABOUT 1⅓ CUPS

¾ cup heavy cream

10 ounces white chocolate, finely chopped

Caramel Frosting

This recipe calls for light brown sugar, but you can substitute dark brown sugar for a more pronounced caramel flavor and color. You will find it included in the Banana-Caramel-Nut Cake Balls on page 55, but feel free to combine it with other types of cake as well.

● ● ●

MAKES ABOUT 1⅓ CUPS

½ cup firmly packed light brown sugar

4 tablespoons (½ stick) unsalted butter, at room temperature, cut into pieces

6 tablespoons whole milk, at room temperature

2 cups sifted confectioners' sugar, plus extra as needed

1　Place the brown sugar, butter, and milk in a small saucepan and stir to combine. Cook over medium heat and bring to a vigorous simmer. Swirl the pot a few times (but do not stir) and simmer for 2 minutes. Remove from the heat and let cool completely.

2　Scrape the cooled caramel into a large bowl and beat with an electric mixer until it thickens and lightens, about 2 minutes. Gradually add 1 cup confectioners' sugar, beating until light and fluffy, about 3 minutes, scraping down the bowl once or twice. Add the remaining 1 cup confectioners' sugar and beat on high speed until silky smooth and spreadable. If the frosting is thinner than you would like, you can add extra confectioners' sugar a tablespoon at a time. The frosting is now ready to use. It is best if used immediately, but it may be refrigerated in an airtight container for up to 4 days. (Bring to room temperature and rebeat before using.)

Lemon Curd

This tart, creamy lemon spread is the best way to bring bright, zesty lemon flavor to your cake balls. It is easy to make and adds a puckery addition to cakes when lemon flavor is desired. The lemon zest adds more flavor, but it also adds texture. If you want your curd to stay silky smooth, leave out the zest.

1 Place the juice, eggs, yolks, and sugar in the top of a double boiler. Whisk briefly to break up the eggs. Add the butter. Place over the bottom of the double boiler filled with enough hot water so that is just touching the bottom of the top pan. Place over medium heat and bring water to a simmer.

2 Whisk the mixture frequently over the simmering water for about 12 minutes, or until the mixture reaches 170°F. (The temperature is more important than the time it takes, and the curd itself should not simmer.) The curd will thicken and form a soft shape when dropped from a spoon. If desired, stir in the zest after removing the mixture from the heat. Let cool to room temperature, scrape into an airtight container, and refrigerate for at least 4 hours, until thoroughly chilled You may store in an airtight container in the refrigerator for up to 1 week.

Note: **You can make this over a low direct heat, without the double boiler, if you whisk it constantly and never leave it for a moment. The risk is that you will scramble the eggs, but if you have a heavy pot and are familiar with making lemon curd, you might give it a try.**

MAKES ABOUT 2 CUPS

½ cup freshly squeezed lemon juice

4 large eggs, at room temperature

2 large egg yolks, at room temperature

1½ cups sugar

12 tablespoons (1½ sticks) unsalted butter, at room temperature, cut into pieces

1 teaspoon finely grated lemon zest (optional)

Pastry Cream

This is a very straightforward version of pastry cream that is easy to make and has a nice vanilla flavor. If there are lumps in your pastry cream when you remove it from the heat, don't panic. Simply press it through a fine-mesh strainer; pastry chefs do it all the time.

● ● ●

MAKES ABOUT 3 CUPS

2½ cups whole milk

½ cup sugar

6 large egg yolks, at room temperature

6 tablespoons all-purpose flour

¼ teaspoon salt

1 tablespoon pure vanilla extract

1 Bring the milk to a boil in a medium pot over medium heat. Remove from the heat and cover to keep warm.

2 Whisk together the sugar and yolks in a medium bowl until creamy. Whisk in the flour and salt, and continue whisking until smooth.

3 Pour about one-quarter of the warm milk over the egg yolk mixture, whisking gently. Add the remaining milk and whisk to combine. Immediately pour the mixture back into the pot and cook over medium-low heat. Whisk almost continuously and watch for bubbles. As soon as the mixture begins to boil, whisk vigorously and cook for 1 to 2 minutes. The pastry cream should be thick enough to mound when dropped from a spoon, but still satiny. Remove from the heat and whisk in the vanilla.

4 Allow the pastry cream to cool. When almost at room temperature, scrape into an airtight container, press plastic wrap directly onto the surface to prevent a skin from forming, cover, and refrigerate for at least 4 hours, or until thoroughly chilled. The pastry cream may be refrigerated for up to 3 days.

Confectioners' Sugar Glaze

Turn to this glaze when you want a lighter coating, such as on a carrot cake, gingerbread, or the Apple Pie Cake Balls on page 50. This recipe provides a veil of sugary, somewhat opaque white glaze. The thicker the glaze, the more opaque it will remain when cooled, but it has to be thin enough to allow you to dip the cake ball. Experiment with the amount of water until you find the consistency you prefer. If you whisk the sugar and water together without heating, the glaze will remain sticky. The best type of rack to use with this recipe has a crisscross pattern of bars, with very small squares created by the bars. This fully supports the cake balls while also allowing the extra glaze to drip off the balls most effectively. The glaze must be made right before using.

Gently whisk together the confectioners' sugar and water in a tall, narrow container. You are aiming for a thick consistency that is just fluid enough for you to dip and coat your cake balls. Add extra water only if necessary. Use immediately.

Note: To dip cake balls into the glaze, line a rimmed baking sheet with parchment paper or aluminum foil. Place a wire rack on top of the lined pan. Using two forks, dip balls one at a time, completely coating them and allowing any excess glaze to drip off. Place on the rack to dry at room temperature. The glaze should be dry to the touch before you store the cake balls, and this might take several hours. Cake balls coated with glaze may be stored overnight at room temperature, loosely covered with aluminum foil.

MAKES ENOUGH TO COAT ABOUT 24 GOLF BALL–SIZE BALLS

4 cups sifted confectioners' sugar

¼ cup water, plus extra as needed

3

The Cake Balls

This chapter showcases complete cake ball creations: versions that are homespun, such as Apple Pie Cake Balls, Carrot Cake Balls, and Red Velvet Cake Balls; sophisticated, such as Crème Brûlée Cake Balls and Chocolate-Orange Grand Marnier Cake Balls; and over-the-top, such as The Crunchie-Munchie, which features chocolate, pretzels, caramel popcorn, and potato chips, and Nutella Cake Balls, which are topped with caramelized hazelnuts. These are my gift to you in a mouthful.

After-Dinner Chocolate-Mint

CAKE BALLS

These were inspired by Andes Crème de Menthe Thins. I love the flavor of these chocolate mints and wondered if I could melt them down to coat a cake ball—it works! Chocolate cake is combined with a peppermint-flavored frosting, rolled into balls, and then dipped in the melted mints. Any mint-flavored desserts tend to be quite aromatic and should be stored separately or else other food items will end up with a minty flavor. If you don't want to melt commercial mints, you can make your own mint chocolate by adding a bit of the peppermint flavoring to melted semisweet, milk, or even white chocolate. See the note for decoration ideas.

1   Beat the peppermint flavoring into the frosting. Combine the cake and about 1 cup of the frosting. Test by compressing and tasting, and add more frosting only if needed for flavor and moisture. Roll into golf ball–size cake balls. Refrigerate until firm. This can be done 1 day ahead; store in an airtight container once they are firm.

2   Line two rimmed baking sheets with parchment paper or aluminum foil. Melt the mints in the microwave or a double boiler. Dip the balls one at a time in the chocolate, encouraging any excess chocolate to drip back into the container. Place, evenly spaced, on the prepared pans. Refrigerate briefly until the chocolate is set. Trim the bottoms, if needed. Place each cake ball in a paper cup, if desired. Place in a single layer in an airtight container and refrigerate for up to 3 days. Bring to room temperature before serving.

Note: Peppermint oils, extracts, and flavorings might all have a peppermint flavor, but they can vary widely in strength. If you cannot find Boyajian peppermint flavoring, start with a smaller amount of another brand of peppermint flavoring, then taste and adjust as needed. For decoration, you can leave as is or pipe a zigzag of white or green melted chocolate or coating. To make these really fancy, place one crystallized mint leaf on each cake ball. Look for these in specialty and gourmet stores.

MAKES ABOUT 52 GOLF BALL–SIZE BALLS

- ½ teaspoon peppermint flavoring, such as Boyajian, or to taste (see the Note)
- ½ batch Confectioners' Sugar Frosting (page 39), ready to use
- 1 batch Super-Easy Chocolate Cake (page 31), baked, cooled, and crumbled
- 6 (4.67-ounce) boxes Andes Crème de Menthe Thins (about 28 mints in each box)
- 52 miniature fluted paper cups (optional)

Apple Pie
CAKE BALLS

There is no pastry crust involved here. Rather, I combine yellow cake with an apple pie filling that you cook from scratch. These are fairly sweet; using some tart apples helps balance the flavors. I have spiced my filling with cinnamon and just a dash of nutmeg, but you can add whatever spices you like in your apple pie. I have offered you three different toppings: a confectionery glaze, chopped walnuts, and cinnamon sugar. The amounts of the toppings suggested assume you will use all three, so adjust accordingly if you want to use only one or two. Read the directions for the Confectioners' Sugar Glaze (page 47) before beginning, to familiarize yourself with that recipe's technique.

**MAKES ABOUT 55
GOLF BALL–SIZE BALLS**

FILLING:

3 Granny Smith apples, peeled, cored, and cut into ¼-inch dice

3 red apples, such as Cortland or McIntosh, peeled, cored, and cut into ¼-inch dice

1 cup sugar

1 teaspoon ground cinnamon

Pinch of nutmeg

2 tablespoons unsalted butter

1   To make the filling: Toss together the apples, sugar, cinnamon, and nutmeg in a bowl until combined. Melt the butter in a large, wide sauté pan. Add the apple mixture and cook over medium heat, stirring occasionally, until the apples are very soft and syrupy, about 10 minutes (you can cover it for part of the time to encourage the cooking). Let cool completely.

2   Line two rimmed baking sheets with parchment paper or aluminum foil; place a cooling rack on one pan. In a small bowl, stir together the sugar and cinnamon for the topping. Place the walnuts on a cutting board. Combine the cake and about three-quarters of the cooked apple mixture. Test by compressing and tasting, and add more apple filling only if needed for flavor and moisture. Roll into golf ball–size cake balls. Refrigerate one-third of the cake balls until firm, about 45 minutes (these will be dipped in glaze). Meanwhile, roll half of the remaining balls in the walnuts and the other half in the cinnamon sugar right away and place on the lined pan.

recipe continues

TOPPINGS:

½ cup sugar

2 teaspoons ground cinnamon

¾ cup toasted walnut halves, finely chopped

1 batch Yellow Buttermilk Cake (page 29), baked, cooled, and crumbled

1 batch Confectioners' Sugar Glaze (page 47), prepared right before using

55 miniature fluted paper cups (optional)

3 Dip the chilled cake balls in the Confectioners' Sugar Glaze, encouraging any excess glaze to drip back into the container. Place, evenly spaced, on the cooling rack. Allow the glazed cake balls to dry at room temperature until the glaze is set. Place each cake ball in a paper cup, if desired. Glazed balls can be placed in a single layer in a container, loosely covered with aluminum foil, and stored at room temperature overnight. Remaining balls with dry toppings can be placed in a single layer in an airtight container and stored at room temperature for up to 2 days.

Note: You could try canned apple pie filling or any other flavor fruit pie filling, although these tend to be sweeter than homemade versions. Depending on the moisture level of the fruit, you would most likely need between 4 and 6 cups of canned filling.

Black Forest

CAKE BALLS

The classic German Black Forest cake combines dark chocolate and cherries, a truly delectable combination. For this cake ball, canned tart cherries are soaked in Kirschwasser (a clear cherry brandy) for an adult kick. You can marinate the cherries as briefly as an hour, but overnight is preferable, so plan ahead. This cake ball will be moist during the rolling step. Make sure each cake ball includes bits of cherries.

● ● ●

1   Chop the drained cherries coarsely. Combine the sugar and water in a small saucepan and stir to combine. Bring to a boil over medium-high heat, swirling the pan once or twice to encourage the sugar to dissolve. Boil for 30 seconds to 1 minute, or until the sugar is dissolved. Let cool and then stir in the Kirschwasser. Add the cherries and let marinate for at least 1 hour or preferably overnight. Drain and discard the liquid.

2   Combine the cake, ¾ cup of the ganache, and the drained cherries. Test by compressing and tasting, and add more ganache only if needed for flavor and moisture. Roll into golf ball–size cake balls. Refrigerate until firm. This can be done 1 day ahead; store in an airtight container once they are firm.

3   Line two rimmed baking sheets with parchment paper or aluminum foil. Melt the chocolate in the microwave or a double boiler. Dip the balls one at a time in the chocolate, encouraging any excess chocolate to drip back into the container. Place, evenly spaced, on the prepared pans. Sprinkle a few pieces of chopped dried cherries on top of each cake ball while the chocolate is still wet. Refrigerate briefly until the chocolate is set. Trim the bottoms, if needed. Place each cake ball in a paper cup, if desired. Place in a single layer in an airtight container and refrigerate for up to 4 days. Bring to room temperature before serving.

MAKES ABOUT 64 GOLF BALL–SIZE BALLS

2 (14.5-ounce) cans tart cherries packed in water, such as Oregon brand, well drained

1 cup sugar

½ cup water

½ cup Kirschwasser

1 batch Super-Easy Chocolate Cake (page 31), baked, cooled, and crumbled

½ batch Dark Chocolate Ganache (page 42), at room temperature, ready to use (should be soft and spreadable)

2 pounds semisweet chocolate, such as Callebaut, Scharffen Berger, or Valrhona Manjari or Equatoriale, finely chopped

1 cup dried tart cherries, chopped

64 miniature fluted paper cups (optional)

Banana-Caramel-Nut

CAKE BALLS

This recipe combines the basic Banana Cake and Caramel Frosting recipes and finishes with a dunk in dark chocolate. I like to decorate the tops of each cake ball with a bit of walnut or banana chips to hint at what is within—your choice. Either way, you need just a small piece of one or the other.

1   Combine the cake and about ¾ cup of the frosting. Test by compressing and tasting, and add more frosting only if needed for flavor and moisture. Roll into golf ball–size cake balls. Refrigerate until firm. This can be done 1 day ahead; store in an airtight container once they are firm.

2   Line two rimmed baking sheets with parchment paper or aluminum foil. Melt the chocolate in the microwave or a double boiler. Dip the balls one at a time in the chocolate, encouraging any excess chocolate to drip back into the container. Place, evenly spaced, on the prepared pans. Place a small piece of walnut or banana chip on top of each cake ball while the chocolate is still wet. Refrigerate briefly, until the chocolate is set. Trim the bottoms, if needed. Place each cake ball in a paper cup, if desired. Place in a single layer in an airtight container and refrigerate for up to 4 days. Bring to room temperature before serving.

Note: The basic Banana Cake also works very well with the Cream Cheese Frosting (page 40). Use 1 batch Banana Cake and about 1 cup Cream Cheese Frosting to create the cake balls.

MAKES ABOUT 52
GOLF BALL–SIZE BALLS

1 batch Banana Cake (page 36), baked, cooled, and crumbled

1 batch Caramel Frosting (page 44), ready to use

1²/₃ pounds semisweet chocolate, such as Callebaut or Ghirardelli, finely chopped

1 cup toasted walnut halves or dried banana chips, chopped or broken into small pieces

52 miniature fluted paper cups (optional)

Boozy
CAKE BALLS

Cake balls made with white, yellow, or chocolate cake can be enhanced by a good soaking with your favorite liqueur or liquor. For examples using specific liquors, turn to Rum Cake Balls (page 120) and Mudslide Cake Balls (page 107). This recipe is meant to be a template for using your favorite booze. Whatever liqueur or liquor you use will be combined with a quantity of sugar and water that have been boiled together. This sugar syrup will help moisten the cake balls and keep the booze evenly distributed; however, the amount of sugar syrup will depend on the alcohol you are using. For instance, if you are using amaretto, which has a high sugar content, you will need less than if you are using bourbon. Just go by taste.

**MAKES ABOUT 52
GOLF BALL–SIZE BALLS**

1 cup sugar

¼ cup water

1 cup liqueur or liquor of your choice, such as Grand Marnier, amaretto, or bourbon

1 batch Yellow Buttermilk Cake (page 29), baked, cooled, and crumbled

1²/3 pounds semisweet or milk chocolate, such as Callebaut, Valrhona, or Scharffen Berger, finely chopped

52 miniature fluted paper cups (optional)

1 Combine the sugar and water in a small saucepan and stir to combine. Bring to a boil over medium-high heat, swirling the pan once or twice to encourage the sugar to dissolve. Boil for 30 seconds to 1 minute, or until the sugar is dissolved. Let cool and then add the liqueur. Place in a large measuring cup or other container with a spout.

2 Place the crumbled cake in a wide bowl (the more surface area the better). Drizzle some of the booze mixture over the cake crumbs, tossing the cake as you go. Your aim is to distribute the liqueur as evenly as possible. Keep pouring and tossing until all of the liquid is absorbed. Now use your hands to thoroughly mix the cake and liquid. Roll into golf ball–size cake balls. Freeze until firm. This can be done 1 day ahead; store in an airtight container once they are firm.

3 Line two rimmed baking sheets with parchment paper or aluminum foil. Melt the chocolate in the microwave or a double boiler. Dip the balls (straight from the freezer) one at a time in the chocolate, encouraging any excess chocolate to drip back into the container. Place, evenly spaced, on the prepared pans. Refrigerate briefly until the chocolate is set. Trim the bottoms, if needed. Place each cake ball in a paper cup, if desired. Place in a single layer in an airtight container and refrigerate for up to 4 days. Bring to room temperature before serving.

Blackout

CAKE BALLS

Ebinger's Blackout Cake was beloved in the metro New York area for many decades of the twentieth century. The bakery closed its doors in the early 1970s, and no one is sure of the original recipe, but it was composed of a very dark chocolate cake layered inside and covered outside by a rich chocolate pudding and then further embellished with an abundant coating of cake crumbs. Here it is turned into a cake ball, with delectable results. You must order black cocoa powder from King Arthur Flour (see Resources, page 165) for these to have the right color and flavor; it is rich and superdark, just like Oreo cookies. (Do not substitute Hershey's Special Dark cocoa powder, as it will not yield the same results.)

1 To make the pudding: Place the cornstarch in a medium pot. Whisk together the milk and cream in a glass measuring cup. Drizzle a few tablespoons of the milk-cream mixture over the cornstarch and whisk until smooth. Pour the remaining milk-cream mixture into the pot, whisking well with cornstarch mixture, then add sugar, unsweetened chocolate, and salt. Cook over low-medium heat, whisking often, until the chocolate melts, then watch carefully as you bring it to a gentle boil. Whisk often as it thickens and takes on a pudding consistency; it should simmer for about 2 minutes. The pudding should be thick and glossy and show whisk marks on top. Remove from the heat and whisk in the vanilla. Scrape into an airtight container and let cool to warm room temperature. Press plastic wrap onto the surface to prevent a skin from forming, snap on the lid, and refrigerate for at least 6 hours or preferably overnight.

2 Crumble the cooled cake. Remove 1 cup of cake crumbs and reserve in an airtight container. Combine the larger amount of crumbled cake with two-thirds of the pudding. Test by compressing and tasting, and add more pudding only if needed for flavor and moisture. Roll into golf ball–size cake balls. Refrigerate until firm. This can be done 1 day ahead; store in an airtight container once they are firm.

recipe continues

MAKES ABOUT 50 GOLF BALL–SIZE BALLS

PUDDING:

3 tablespoons sifted cornstarch

1½ cups whole milk

¾ cup heavy cream

1 cup minus 1 tablespoon sugar

4½ ounces unsweetened chocolate, finely chopped, such as Scharffen Berger 99%

Pinch of salt

1⅛ teaspoons pure vanilla extract

1 batch Super-Easy Chocolate Cake (page 31), made with ⅓ cup black cocoa powder (see headnote) and ⅓ cup natural cocoa powder

1²/₃ pounds semisweet chocolate, such as Callebaut or Valrhona Equatoriale, finely chopped

50 miniature fluted paper cups (optional)

3   Line two rimmed baking sheets with parchment paper or aluminum foil. Melt the semisweet chocolate in the microwave or a double boiler. Dip the balls one at a time in the chocolate, encouraging any excess chocolate to drip back into the container. Place, evenly spaced, on the prepared pans. Sprinkle some of the cake crumbs on top of each cake ball while the chocolate is still wet. Refrigerate briefly until the chocolate is set. Trim the bottoms, if needed. Place each cake ball in a paper cup, if desired. Place in a single layer in an airtight container and refrigerate for up to 3 days. Bring to room temperature before serving.

Boston Cream

CAKE BALLS

Fans of Boston cream pie know that it is a classic dessert featuring yellow cake, vanilla pastry cream, and a chocolate glaze—the perfect combo for a cake ball. With many cake balls, you add only enough binder to hold the ball together. This is one cake ball where you want to add as much binder—pastry cream in this case—as possible to create the velvety texture that only pastry cream can provide.

**MAKES ABOUT 72
GOLF BALL-SIZE BALLS**

1 batch Super-Easy Yellow Cake (page 30), baked, cooled, and crumbled

1 batch Pastry Cream (page 46), chilled and ready to use

2½ pounds semisweet chocolate, such as Callebaut or Ghirardelli, finely chopped

72 miniature fluted paper cups (optional)

1   Combine the cake and about 2 cups of the pastry cream. Test by compressing, and add as much additional pastry cream as the cake will hold. Roll into golf ball-size cake balls. Refrigerate until firm. This can be done 1 day ahead; store in an airtight container once they are firm.

2   Line two rimmed baking sheets with parchment paper or aluminum foil. Melt the chocolate in the microwave or a double boiler. Remove about ¼ cup of the melted chocolate and set aside. Dip the balls one at a time in the larger amount of chocolate, encouraging any excess chocolate to drip back into the container, and place, evenly spaced, on the prepared pans.

3   Place the reserved melted chocolate in a parchment cone (see page 25), snip a small opening from the tip, and pipe a design of your choice on top of each cake ball, if desired. Refrigerate briefly until the chocolate is set. Trim the bottoms, if needed. Place each cake ball in a paper cup, if desired. Place in a single layer in an airtight container and refrigerate for up to 3 days. Bring to room temperature before serving.

Cappuccino
CAKE BALLS

The flavors from your favorite indulgent coffeehouse treat come together in this cake ball: yellow cake enhanced with freshly ground coffee; espresso frosting; a dunk in your choice of semisweet, white, or milk chocolate; and a dusting of cinnamon and cocoa on top. You will need both freshly ground coffee and instant espresso powder for this recipe. To help the espresso powder dissolve in the milk for the frosting, warm the milk first.

1 Crumble the cooled cake and combine with 1½ cups of the espresso frosting. Test by compressing and tasting, and add more frosting only if needed for flavor and moisture. Roll into golf ball–size cake balls. Refrigerate until firm. This can be done 1 day ahead; store in an airtight container once they are firm.

2 Line two rimmed baking sheets with parchment paper or aluminum foil. Stir together the cinnamon and cocoa powder in a small bowl. Melt the chocolate in the microwave or a double boiler. Dip the balls one at a time in the chocolate, encouraging any excess chocolate to drip back into the container. Place, evenly spaced, on the prepared pans. Sprinkle a bit of the cinnamon-cocoa mixture on top of each cake ball while the chocolate is still wet. Refrigerate briefly until the chocolate is set. Trim the bottoms, if needed. Place each cake ball in a paper cup, if desired. Place in a single layer in an airtight container and refrigerate for up to 4 days. Bring to room temperature before serving.

Note: **To make this more of a Mochaccino Cake Ball, use Fudgy Chocolate Frosting (page 41) in lieu of Confectioners' Sugar Frosting, dissolving the 1 tablespoon instant espresso powder in the warmed milk for the chocolate frosting.**

MAKES ABOUT 70 GOLF BALL–SIZE BALLS

- 1 batch Yellow Buttermilk Cake (page 29), made with 1 tablespoon plus 1 teaspoon finely ground coffee added to the batter along with the vanilla extract
- 1 batch Confectioners' Sugar Frosting (page 39), made with 1 tablespoon instant espresso powder added to the milk, ready to use
- 1½ teaspoons ground cinnamon
- 1½ teaspoons natural cocoa powder
- 2¼ pounds Callebaut or Valrhona semisweet, white, or milk chocolate, or Ghirardelli semisweet or milk chocolate, finely chopped
- 70 miniature fluted paper cups (optional)

Carrot Cake 'n' Cream Cheese Frosting

CAKE BALLS

I have listed the Carrot Cake in the Basics section because it really is a cake that can be combined with a variety of frostings and fillings; however, I still love it best of all when paired with Cream Cheese Frosting. You can dip the balls in chocolate, or try the Confectioners' Sugar Glaze. Here I suggest a fancy finish with a dip in white chocolate, chocolate cookie crumb "dirt" sprinkled on top, and a sugar carrot "planted" in each cake ball.

1   Combine the cake with ¾ cup of the frosting. Test by compressing and tasting, and add more frosting only if needed for flavor and moisture. Roll into golf ball–size cake balls. Refrigerate until firm. This can be done 1 day ahead; store in an airtight container once they are firm.

2   Line two rimmed baking sheets with parchment paper or aluminum foil. Melt the chocolate in the microwave or a double boiler. Dip the balls one at a time in the chocolate, encouraging any excess chocolate to drip back into the container. Place, evenly spaced, on the prepared pans. Sprinkle a bit of cookie crumbs, if desired, on top of each cake ball while the chocolate is still wet. Insert a sugar carrot, if desired, into the center of the cookie crumbs by pressing the carrot down into the cake ball so that the carrot "top" is still exposed. Refrigerate briefly until the chocolate is set. Trim the bottoms, if needed. Place each cake ball in a paper cup, if desired. Place in a single layer in an airtight container and refrigerate for up to 4 days. Bring to room temperature before serving.

**MAKES ABOUT 58
GOLF BALL–SIZE BALLS**

1 batch Carrot Cake (page 35), baked, cooled, and crumbled

½ batch Cream Cheese Frosting (page 40), ready to use

2 pounds white chocolate, such as Callebaut or Valrhona Ivoire, finely chopped

⅓ cup finely crushed dark chocolate cookie crumbs (from cookies such as Nabisco Famous Chocolate Wafers; optional)

58 molded sugar carrots (see Resources, page 165; optional)

58 miniature fluted paper cups (optional)

Chocolate-Cherry

CAKE BALLS

Chocolate-covered cherries are a classic gift for midwinter holidays. This cake ball combines chocolate cake, tart cherry preserves, chocolate ganache, and a dip in dark chocolate for a new take on the candy classic. The choice of decoration is up to you, but I have suggested two elegant approaches: tiny edible metallic hearts and free-form painting with edible gold. See Resources (pages 165 and 166) for information.

● ● ●

**MAKES ABOUT 64
GOLF BALL–SIZE BALLS**

1 batch Super-Easy Chocolate Cake (page 31), baked, cooled, and crumbled

½ batch Dark Chocolate Ganache (page 42), made with Valrhona Equatoriale, at room temperature, ready to use (should be soft and spreadable)

¾ cup tart cherry preserves

2 pounds bittersweet or semisweet chocolate, such as Valrhona Guanaja, Caraïbe, or Equatoriale, finely chopped

Wilton edible metallic pink hearts

Edible gold powder

Vodka or pure almond extract

Small artist's brush

64 miniature fluted paper cups (optional)

1   Combine the cake with ¾ cup of the ganache and all of the preserves. Test by compressing and tasting, and add more ganache only if needed for flavor and moisture. Roll into golf ball–size cake balls. Refrigerate until firm. This can be done 1 day ahead; store in an airtight container once they are firm.

2   Line two rimmed baking sheets with parchment paper or aluminum foil. Melt the chocolate in the microwave or a double boiler. Dip the balls one at a time in the chocolate, encouraging any excess chocolate to drip back into the container. Place, evenly spaced, on the prepared pans. Sprinkle a few metallic hearts on top of half of the cake balls while the chocolate is still wet. Refrigerate all the cake balls briefly until the chocolate is set. Trim the bottoms, if needed.

3   For the cake balls that are still unadorned, decorate as follows: Place about ½ teaspoon of gold powder in a small bowl. Add a few drops of vodka or almond extract and stir with the brush, adding only enough liquid to reach a paint-like consistency. Paint free-form gold shapes or designs on the chilled cake balls. The paint will dry almost immediately. Place each cake ball in a paper cup, if desired. Place in a single layer in an airtight container and refrigerate for up to 3 days. Bring to room temperature before serving.

Chocolate-Orange Grand Marnier
CAKE BALLS

These are strictly adult fare: chocolaty, with a serious dose of Grand Marnier liqueur and fresh orange zest in the cake batter and minced, chewy candied orange zest both inside and on top. They are fabulous as a host or hostess gift.

1 Crumble the cooled cake and combine with ¾ cup of the ganache, ⅔ cup of the candied zest, and the Grand Marnier. Test by compressing and tasting, and add more ganache only if needed for flavor and moisture. Roll into golf ball–size cake balls. Refrigerate until firm. This can be done 1 day ahead; store in an airtight container once they are firm.

2 Line two rimmed baking sheets with parchment paper or aluminum foil. Melt the chocolate in the microwave or a double boiler. Dip the balls one at a time in the chocolate, encouraging any excess chocolate to drip back into the container. Place, evenly spaced, on the prepared pans. Sprinkle a few pieces of reserved candied zest on top of each cake ball while the chocolate is still wet. Refrigerate briefly until the chocolate is set. Trim the bottoms, if needed. Place each cake ball in a paper cup, if desired. Place in a single layer in an airtight container and refrigerate for up to 4 days. Bring to room temperature before serving.

MAKES ABOUT 60 GOLF BALL–SIZE BALLS

- 1 batch Super-Easy Chocolate Cake (page 31), made with 2 teaspoons freshly grated orange zest added along with the vanilla extract
- ½ batch Dark Chocolate Ganache (page 42), at room temperature, ready to use (should be soft and spreadable)
- 1 cup candied orange zest, finely minced
- 1 cup Grand Marnier
- 2 pounds semisweet chocolate, such as Callebaut or Valrhona Manjari or Equatoriale, finely chopped
- 60 miniature fluted paper cups (optional)

Cassata

CAKE BALLS

Cassata is a classic Sicilian cake that has many versions, but often it combines a fairly simple sponge cake with fresh ricotta, candied orange peel, liqueur, and shavings of chocolate. This cake ball features all of these traditional flavors. Make sure to use fresh ricotta for its incomparable flavor, which you will probably have to locate at a cheese or specialty store. Regular supermarket ricotta, which has a different water content, will not work here. Maraschino liqueur has flavors of cherry and bitter almond and brings everything together in this sophisticated, adult cake ball. The ingredient list is long, but you can make the nut brittle for the topping ahead of time.

● ● ●

**MAKES ABOUT 62
GOLF BALL–SIZE BALLS**

NUT BRITTLE:

¼ cup sugar

2½ teaspoons water

⅓ cup blanched almonds, coarsely chopped

FILLING:

¼ cup sugar

¼ cup water

½ cup maraschino liqueur, such as Luxardo

½ cup plus 3 tablespoons dried tart cherries, minced

½ cup plus 3 tablespoons minced candied orange peel

1   To make the nut brittle: Line a rimmed baking sheet with parchment paper or aluminum foil. Stir the sugar and water together in a small saucepan. Bring to a simmer over medium-high heat, swirling the pan once or twice, but do not stir. Cook until the sugar is caramelized and has turned a medium golden brown. Stir in the almonds until coated, then immediately scrape out onto the prepared pan. Let cool; the brittle will harden. Break off pieces of nut brittle, place on a cutting board, and use a large chef's knife to chop finely. This can be done up to 4 days ahead; store in an airtight container at room temperature.

2   To make the filling: Combine the sugar and water in a saucepan and stir to combine. Bring to a boil over medium-high heat, swirling the pan once or twice to encourage the sugar to dissolve. Boil for 30 seconds to 1 minute, or until the sugar is dissolved. Let cool and then add the liqueur. Stir in ½ cup of the cherries and ½ cup of the orange peel and allow to marinate for at least 15 minutes.

recipe continues

1 (1½-ounce) block semisweet or bittersweet chocolate, such as Scharffen Berger semisweet or Valrhona Manjari

1 batch White Cake (page 34), baked, cooled, and crumbled

1½ cups fresh ricotta cheese

6 tablespoons sifted confectioners' sugar

2 pounds semisweet or bittersweet chocolate, such as Scharffen Berger semisweet or Valrhona Manjari, finely chopped

62 miniature fluted paper cups (optional)

3 Grate the 1½-ounce block of chocolate on the largest holes of a box grater. Toss the grated chocolate with the crumbled cake until distributed evenly. Use a slotted spoon to remove the fruit from the liqueur and toss into the cake mixture. Drizzle the liqueur over the cake and toss to distribute evenly. Whisk together the ricotta and confectioners' sugar in a small bowl until smooth. Add 1¼ cups of the ricotta mixture to the cake mixture. Test by compressing and tasting, and add more ricotta only if needed for flavor and moisture. Roll into golf ball–size cake balls. Refrigerate until firm. This can be done 1 day ahead; store in an airtight container once they are firm.

4 Line two rimmed baking sheets with parchment paper or aluminum foil. Toss together the chopped nut brittle and the remaining 3 tablespoons cherries and 3 tablespoons orange peel for the decorative topping. Melt the chocolate in the microwave or a double boiler. Dip the balls one at a time in the chocolate, encouraging any excess chocolate to drip back into the container. Place, evenly spaced, on the prepared pans. Sprinkle a bit of the topping on top of each cake ball while the chocolate is still wet. Refrigerate briefly until the chocolate is set. Trim the bottoms, if needed. Place each cake ball in a paper cup, if desired. Place in a single layer in an airtight container and refrigerate for up to 3 days. Bring to room temperature before serving.

Chocolate Chip Cookie Dough

CAKE BALLS

Okay, I know I am stretching the definition of "cake" here, but there are a lot of raw cookie dough eaters out there, and this recipe is for you (and me)! It is a classic Toll House chocolate chip cookie dough, minus the egg, with a bit of milk added for moistness. Also, while we don't need the baking soda for leavening, it does add a certain taste that we look for in raw dough, so it is in there, but in a reduced amount. I suggest making these in a smaller 1-inch size, as they are quite sweet and rich. Yes, this makes a large batch, but they freeze well and will be eaten quite quickly.

● ● ●

1 Whisk the flour, salt, and baking soda together in a bowl to aerate and combine; set aside.

2 In a large bowl with an electric mixer on medium-high speed, beat the butter until creamy, about 2 minutes. Gradually add the sugars, beating until light and fluffy, about 3 minutes, scraping down the bowl once or twice; beat in the milk and vanilla. Add about one-third of the flour mixture and mix on low speed. Gradually add the remaining flour mixture, mixing just until blended. Beat in 1¾ cups of the morsels. Cover the bowl with plastic wrap and refrigerate for about 1 hour, or until firm enough to roll. (You may freeze the dough for up to 1 month; defrost in the refrigerator overnight before proceeding.) Roll the cookie dough into 1-inch balls and refrigerate until firm.

3 Line two rimmed baking sheets with parchment paper or aluminum foil. Melt the chopped chocolate in the microwave or a double boiler. Dip the balls one at a time in the chocolate, encouraging any excess chocolate to drip back into the container. Place, evenly spaced, on the prepared pans. Place a single reserved chocolate morsel on top of each cake ball while the chocolate is still wet. Refrigerate briefly until the chocolate is set. Trim the bottoms, if needed. Place each ball in a paper cup, if desired. Place in a single layer in an airtight container and refrigerate for up to 5 days. Bring to room temperature before serving.

MAKES ABOUT 100 1-INCH CAKE BALLS

2½ cups all-purpose flour

1 teaspoon salt

¼ teaspoon baking soda

1 cup (2 sticks) unsalted butter, at room temperature, cut into pieces

¾ cup granulated sugar

¾ cup firmly light packed brown sugar

2 tablespoons whole milk

1 teaspoon pure vanilla extract

2 cups (one 12-ounce package) mini semisweet chocolate morsels

25 ounces semisweet chocolate, such as Callebaut or Ghirardelli, finely chopped

100 (1-inch) fluted paper cups (sometimes labeled as candy cups; optional)

Chocolate Tempering

INSTRUCTIONS

*A*lways use high-quality chocolate that has a high cocoa butter content when tempering. I recommend Valrhona and Scharffen Berger brands. Tempering is not difficult, but it does take time and you must be precise. You will need a chocolate thermometer, which has 1-degree increments in a range from 40° to 130°F.

Start with the amount of chocolate called for in the recipe and chop it very finely.

Place about two-thirds of the chopped chocolate in the top of a double boiler with gently simmering water in the lower half of the double boiler. The water should not touch the bottom of the pot holding the chocolate.

Stir gently to encourage melting, but not vigorously, which will add air.

Do not allow chocolate to heat above 115°F for bittersweet and semisweet chocolate and 110°F for white or milk chocolate. As soon as the chocolate is almost completely melted, remove the pot from the heat and wipe the bottom of the pot to eliminate any chance of water droplets reaching the chocolate, which would cause it to seize.

Add about one-third of the remaining chopped chocolate and stir gently. The residual heat will melt it. You want to cool the chocolate down to 79°F.

Add the remaining chocolate, in two more stages if necessary, to cool the chocolate further, continuing to stir gently until 79°F is reached.

Place the pot back over hot, but not simmering, water, and rewarm gently. Bittersweet and semisweet chocolates should be brought up to 88° to 90°F, milk chocolate to 85° to 88°F, and white chocolate to 84° to 87°F. Do not allow any chocolate to rise above 90°F or you will have to begin the entire process again.

The chocolate is now ready to use.

To test the temper, thinly spread a teaspoonful on a piece of aluminum foil and allow it to cool. If your room temperature is warm, refrigerate it for about 2 minutes. The chocolate should look shiny and smooth and break with a crisp snap. Any dull spots or streaks, or a soft texture, indicate that the chocolate is not in good temper.

Now you must maintain the chocolate's temperature while you are working with it. Try setting a heating pad on low and placing your bowl of tempered chocolate on top of it. If you have a warming tray, you may use that instead.

Always keep checking the temperature, keeping it within its range. Stir it occasionally to keep the entire amount evenly heated, as it will cool around the edges.

Cocoa-Dusted Truffle

CAKE BALLS

A truffle and a cake ball rolled (literally) into one. Moist chocolate cake is combined with a dark chocolate ganache, which is what is found in a truffle center. The cake balls are dipped in a chocolate shell and embellished with a dusting of cocoa—just like a truffle. You can dip these balls in simple melted chocolate, or you can temper the chocolate so that the outer chocolate shell will be crisp and shiny just like an actual truffle candy. See the sidebar on page 70 for these directions. (You may temper chocolate for any of the cake balls in the book that are coated with chocolate, if you would like this effect.)

● ● ●

1   Combine the cake and about 1½ cups of the ganache. Test by compressing and add as much of the remaining ganache as the cake will hold. Roll into golf ball–size cake balls. Refrigerate until firm. This can be done 1 day ahead; store in an airtight container once they are firm.

2   Line two rimmed baking sheets with parchment paper or aluminum foil. Melt the chocolate in the microwave or a double boiler, or temper the chocolate as described in the sidebar. Dip the balls one at a time, encouraging any excess chocolate to drip back into the container. Place, evenly spaced, on the prepared pans. Use a fine-mesh strainer to sift a generous coating of cocoa on top of each cake ball while the chocolate is still wet. Refrigerate briefly until the chocolate is set. Trim the bottoms, if needed. Place each cake ball in a paper cup, if desired. Place in a single layer in an airtight container and refrigerate for up to 3 days. Bring to room temperature before serving.

Note: The choice of chocolates used for your ganache and for your chocolate shell will make or break this cake ball. Use the very best-quality chocolate you can afford. I really like making the ganache with Valrhona Equatoriale and then using a darker, more bittersweet Valrhona for the shell, such as Caraïbe (66 percent), Guanaja (70 percent), or even Manjari (64 percent), which is very fruity and complex.

MAKES ABOUT 64 GOLF BALL–SIZE BALLS

1 batch Super-Easy Chocolate Cake (page 31), baked, cooled, and crumbled

1 batch Dark Chocolate Ganache (page 42), made with Valrhona Equatoriale, at room temperature, ready to use (should be soft and spreadable)

2 pounds bittersweet or semisweet chocolate, such as Valrhona Guanaja, Caraïbe, or Equatoriale, finely chopped

Natural or Dutch-processed cocoa powder, for dusting

64 miniature fluted paper cups (optional)

Chocolate-Raspberry

CAKE BALLS

These are dark, luscious, and sophisticated—very much like a cross between a bite of cake and an elegant truffle. The rich chocolate flavor of the cake, the fruity chocolate ganache, and the tangy burst of fresh berries make this a must-try cake ball for adults with a sophisticated palate. Use the chocolates suggested for the best results. To purchase freeze-dried raspberries, check your local Whole Foods Market or see Resources (page 164) for the company Just Tomatoes, Etc.!

**MAKES ABOUT 70
GOLF BALL–SIZE BALLS**

1 batch Super-Easy Chocolate Cake (page 31), baked, cooled, and crumbled

3 cups fresh raspberries

½ batch Dark Chocolate Ganache (page 42), made with Valrhona Manjari or Scharffen Berger semisweet, at room temperature, ready to use (should be soft and spreadable)

2¼ pounds dark chocolate, such as Valrhona Manjari or Scharffen Berger semisweet, finely chopped

½ cup freeze-dried raspberries, crushed

70 miniature fluted paper cups (optional)

1   Combine the cake and fresh berries, using a pastry blender to break down the berries. Add ⅔ cup of the ganache. Test by compressing and tasting, and add more ganache only if needed for flavor and moisture. Roll into golf ball–size cake balls. Refrigerate until firm. This can be done 1 day ahead; store in an airtight container once they are firm.

2   Line two rimmed baking sheets with parchment paper or aluminum foil. Melt the chocolate in the microwave or a double boiler. Dip the balls one at a time in the chocolate, encouraging any excess chocolate to drip back into the container. Place, evenly spaced, on the prepared pans. Sprinkle a bit of the crushed freeze-dried raspberries on top of each cake ball while the chocolate is still wet. Refrigerate briefly until the chocolate is set. Trim the bottoms, if needed. Place each cake ball in a paper cup, if desired. Place in a single layer in an airtight container and refrigerate for up to 3 days. Bring to room temperature before serving.

Note: I have also made these with the addition of some Chambord liqueur sprinkled over the cake before mixing in the fresh berries and ganache. Just take care not to make the mixture too wet.

Coffee
CAKE BALLS

Perfect for a mid-morning office break or a brunch buffet, these cake balls combine a sour cream coffee cake with walnut- and cinnamon-scented streusel.

1 To make the streusel: Stir together all the streusel ingredients until combined; set aside.

2 Position a rack in the middle of the oven. Preheat the oven to 350°F. Coat the inside of a 9 x 13-inch rectangular pan with nonstick cooking spray; set aside. Line a rimmed baking sheet with parchment paper or aluminum foil; set aside.

3 To make the cake: Whisk together the flour, baking powder, baking soda, and salt in a medium bowl to aerate and combine; set aside.

4 In a large bowl with an electric mixer on medium-high speed, beat the butter until creamy, about 2 minutes. Gradually add the sugar and beat until very light and fluffy, about 3 minutes, scraping down the bowl once or twice. Beat in the vanilla until thoroughly combined.

5 Beat in the eggs one at a time, scraping down the bowl after each addition and allowing each egg to be absorbed before continuing. Add the flour mixture in four additions, alternating with the sour cream. Begin and end with the flour mixture and beat briefly until smooth. Pour the batter into the prepared rectangular pan. Sprinkle ¾ cup of the streusel onto the prepared baking sheet. Sprinkle the remaining streusel evenly all over the coffee cake batter.

recipe continues

**MAKES ABOUT 42
GOLF BALL–SIZE BALLS**

STREUSEL:

⅔ cup all-purpose flour

⅔ cup firmly packed light brown sugar

½ cup toasted walnut halves, finely chopped

4 tablespoons (½ stick) unsalted butter, melted

1 teaspoon ground cinnamon

⅛ teaspoon salt

CAKE:

2 cups all-purpose flour

1 teaspoon baking powder

1 teaspoon baking soda

½ teaspoon salt

4 tablespoons (½ stick) unsalted butter, at room temperature, cut into pieces

¾ cup granulated sugar

2 teaspoons pure vanilla extract

2 large eggs, at room
temperature

1¼ cups sour cream or
buttermilk

½ batch Cream Cheese
Frosting (page 40), ready
to use

1⅓ pounds white
chocolate, such as
Callebaut or Valrhona
Ivoire, finely chopped

42 miniature fluted paper
cups

6   Bake both pans for about 10 minutes and then check the streusel-
only pan. It should be light golden brown (it might take about 12 minutes total). Remove the streusel-only pan and let cool on a wire rack.
The cake will take about 25 minutes total, or until a toothpick inserted
in the center shows a few moist crumbs when removed. Cool the cake
completely in the pan on a rack. The cake is ready to use. Alternatively,
double-wrap the pan in plastic wrap and store at room temperature for
up to 1 day before proceeding; the streusel can also be stored in an airtight container at room temperature for up to 1 day before proceeding.

7   Crumble the cooled cake and combine with ¾ cup of the frosting.
Test by compressing and tasting, and add more frosting only if needed
for flavor and moisture. Roll into golf ball–size cake balls. Refrigerate
until firm. This can be done 1 day ahead; store in an airtight container
once they are firm.

8   Line two rimmed baking sheets with parchment paper or aluminum
foil. Melt the chocolate in the microwave or a double boiler. Dip the
balls one at a time in the chocolate, encouraging any excess chocolate
to drip back into the container. Place, evenly spaced, on the prepared
pans. Sprinkle some of the reserved streusel on top of each cake ball
while the chocolate is still wet. Refrigerate briefly until the chocolate is
set. Trim the bottoms, if needed. Place each cake ball in a paper cup, if
desired. Place in a single layer in an airtight container and refrigerate
for up to 2 days. Bring to room temperature before serving.

Coconut-Chocolate

CAKE BALLS

When you shop for ingredients, make sure to buy pure unsweetened coconut milk and not sweetened condensed coconut milk. The technique of reducing the coconut milk concentrates its flavor to the maximum; to further highlight the flavor, it is used in both the cake and the filling. You can find pure coconut milk in many large supermarkets and most Asian supermarkets; note that the can weight can vary by a few ounces, which is okay. Dip half of the balls in white chocolate and half in semisweet chocolate; the latter option gives you the cake ball equivalent of a Mounds candy bar. You will need a candy thermometer for this recipe.

MAKES ABOUT 80 GOLF BALL–SIZE BALLS

2 (14-ounce) cans pure unsweetened coconut milk

FILLING:

8 large egg yolks

1⅓ cups sugar

⅔ cup reduced coconut milk (from above)

1¾ cups (3½ sticks) unsalted butter, at room temperature, cut into pieces

5⅓ cups sweetened long-shred coconut

1   Pour both cans of coconut milk into a wide saucepan and bring to a simmer over medium heat (you might need a splatter shield). Simmer until reduced by half, 5 to 10 minutes; it will be visibly thickened. Let cool completely. You may refrigerate this in an airtight container for up to 3 days. Bring to room temperature before proceeding.

2   To make the filling: In a large bowl with an electric mixer on high speed, beat the egg yolks until thick and creamy. Stir the sugar and ⅔ cup reduced coconut milk together in a saucepan and bring to a simmer over medium heat. Simmer, whisking occasionally, until the mixture reaches 238°F on a candy thermometer. Pour a couple of tablespoons of the hot coconut milk mixture over the egg yolks and start beating on high speed. Slowly drizzle the remaining coconut milk mixture over the egg yolks, continuing to beat until cool to the touch (this will take a few minutes). Beat in the butter, a few tablespoons at a time, until the mixture is creamy and smooth. Fold in the 5⅓ cups shredded coconut. You may refrigerate the filling in an airtight container for up to 3 days. Bring to room temperature before proceeding.

3 Crumble the cooled cake and combine with three-quarters of the coconut filling. Test by compressing and tasting, and add more coconut filling only if needed for flavor and moisture. Roll into golf ball–size cake balls. Refrigerate until firm. This can be done 1 day ahead; store in an airtight container once they are firm.

4 Line two rimmed baking sheets with parchment paper or aluminum foil. Melt both chocolates separately in the microwave or double boilers. Dip half the balls in the white chocolate and half the balls in the semisweet chocolate, one at a time, encouraging any excess chocolate to drip back into the container. Place, evenly spaced, on the prepared pans. Sprinkle a bit of shredded coconut on top of each cake ball while the chocolate is still wet. Refrigerate briefly until the chocolate is set. Trim the bottoms, if needed. Place each cake ball in a paper cup, if desired. Place in a single layer in an airtight container and refrigerate for up to 4 days. Bring to room temperature before serving.

1 batch Yellow Buttermilk Cake (page 29), made using 1¼ cups of the reduced coconut milk (from above) instead of buttermilk

1¼ pounds white chocolate, such as Callebaut or Valrhona Ivoire, finely chopped

1¼ pounds semisweet chocolate, such as Callebaut, Ghirardelli, or Valrhona Equatoriale, finely chopped

1⅓ cups sweetened long-shred coconut

80 miniature fluted paper cups (optional)

Confetti

CAKE BALLS

Whether you call them rainbow sprinkles or jimmies (as we do here in New England), you are probably used to seeing these tiny sugar embellishments on top of ice cream cones or cupcakes as decoration. In recent years, they have become very popular baked into white cake batter to create a colorful, speckled effect. There are even cake mixes that include the sprinkles. Additional sprinkles can be added to the top of the white chocolate–dipped cake ball, or you can use Wilton Colorburst Candy Melts, which have specks of color right in the chocolate coating.

●　　●　　●

1　Crumble the cooled cake and combine with ¾ cup of the frosting. Test by compressing and tasting, and add more frosting only if needed for flavor and moisture. Roll into golf ball–size cake balls. Refrigerate until firm. This can be done 1 day ahead; store in an airtight container once they are firm.

2　Line two rimmed baking sheets with parchment paper or aluminum foil. Melt the chocolate in the microwave or a double boiler. Dip the balls one at a time in the chocolate, encouraging any excess chocolate to drip back into the container. Place, evenly spaced, on the prepared pans. Scatter some of the sprinkles on top of each cake ball while the chocolate is still wet. Refrigerate briefly until the chocolate is set. Trim the bottoms, if needed. Place each cake ball in a paper cup, if desired. Place in a single layer in an airtight container and refrigerate for up to 3 days. Bring to room temperature before serving.

MAKES ABOUT 46 GOLF BALL–SIZE BALLS

- 1 batch White Cake (page 34), made with ¼ cup rainbow sprinkles folded into the batter before baking
- ½ batch Confectioners' Sugar Frosting (page 39), ready to use
- 1½ pounds white chocolate, such as Callebaut or Valrhona Ivoire, finely chopped
- ¼ cup rainbow sprinkles
- 46 miniature fluted paper cups (optional)

Cranberry-Toffee-Walnut
CAKE BALLS

Sometimes an unusual combination of flavors ends up being more than the sum of its parts. Tart dried cranberries combined with toffee bits, toasted walnuts, dark chocolate cake, and milk chocolate ganache equal one decadent cake ball. Dip half the batch in milk chocolate and half in semisweet, and sprinkle all of them with additional cranberries, toffee, and nuts. This is perfect for holiday gift giving.

● ● ●

MAKES ABOUT 64 GOLF BALL–SIZE BALLS

1 batch Super-Easy Chocolate Cake (page 31), baked, cooled, and crumbled

½ batch Milk Chocolate Ganache (page 43), at room temperature, ready to use (should be soft and spreadable)

2⅓ cups dried cranberries, chopped

2¼ cups toasted walnut halves, finely chopped

2¼ cups toffee bits, such as Heath Bits 'O Brickle

1 pound milk chocolate, such as Callebaut or Valrhona Jivara, finely chopped

1 pound semisweet chocolate, such as Callebaut or Valrhona Equatoriale, finely chopped

64 miniature fluted paper cups (optional)

1 Combine the cake with ¾ cup of the ganache, 1 cup of the cranberries, ⅔ cup of the nuts, and ⅔ cup of the toffee bits. Test by compressing and tasting, and add more ganache only if needed for flavor and moisture. Roll into golf ball–size cake balls. Refrigerate until firm. This can be done 1 day ahead; store in an airtight container once they are firm.

2 Line two rimmed baking sheets with parchment paper or aluminum foil. Toss together the remaining cranberries, nuts, and toffee bits. Melt the milk and semisweet chocolates separately in the microwave or double boilers. Dip the balls one at a time (half of the balls in each flavor), encouraging any excess chocolate to drip back into the container. Place, evenly spaced, on the prepared pans. Sprinkle a generous amount of the mixed topping on each cake ball while the chocolate is still wet. Refrigerate briefly until the chocolate is set. Trim the bottoms, if needed. Place each cake ball in a paper cup, if desired. Place in a single layer in an airtight container and refrigerate for up to 4 days. Bring to room temperature before serving.

Note: For a fabulous variation, substitute dried cherries for the cranberries and substitute finely chopped blanched almonds for the walnuts.

Cranberry–White Chocolate

CAKE BALLS

Perfect for the fall and winter months, this cake ball combines white cake, cranberry sauce, white chocolate, and dried cranberries. While the recipe recommends canned whole cranberry sauce (not jellied), this is simply a time-saver suggestion. If you have a recipe for a classic cranberry sauce using whole berries (such as the one often found right on the bag), by all means make it and use it. You will need about 3 cups of cranberry sauce.

● ● ●

1 Combine the cake and 2 cups of the cranberry sauce. Mix until the cake and cranberry sauce are thoroughly combined. Test by compressing and tasting, and add more cranberry sauce only if needed for flavor and moisture. Roll into golf ball–size cake balls. Refrigerate until firm. This can be done 1 day ahead; store in an airtight container once they are firm.

2 Line two rimmed baking sheets with parchment paper or aluminum foil. Use a large chef's knife to make small shards of chocolate to equal about ½ cup. Toss these chocolate shavings with the dried cranberries. Melt the remaining chocolate in the microwave or a double boiler. Dip the balls one at a time in the chocolate, encouraging any excess chocolate to drip back into the container. Place, evenly spaced, on the prepared pans. Sprinkle a bit of the white chocolate–cranberry mixture on top of each cake ball while the chocolate is still wet. Refrigerate briefly until the chocolate is set. Trim the bottoms, if needed. Place each cake ball in a paper cup, if desired. Place in a single layer in an airtight container and refrigerate for up to 4 days. Bring to room temperature before serving.

Note: I like to use Ocean Spray Craisins, as they are a vivid red color. You can often find dried cranberries in bulk, but typically they are not as visually appealing, in my opinion.

MAKES ABOUT 72
GOLF BALL–SIZE BALLS

1 batch White Cake (page 34), baked, cooled, and crumbled

3 cups homemade cranberry sauce (using whole cranberries), or 2 (14-ounce) cans whole cranberry sauce (not jellied), such as Ocean Spray

2⅓ pounds bulk white chocolate, such as Callebaut or Valrhona Ivoire

1 cup dried cranberries, chopped

72 miniature fluted paper cups (optional)

Crème Brûlée

CAKE BALLS

These are utterly exquisite, if I do say so myself. First you prepare a rich custard, as though you were making a crème brûlée. Once chilled, it is combined with white cake and rolled into balls. After chilling, the balls are dipped in a deeply golden caramelized sugar mixture. Stunning. This is what my pastry chef daughter calls "advanced balling"; there are a few unusual techniques employed, but the results are show-stopping. Please read the recipe through before starting in order to acquaint yourself with the entire process. For this recipe, the fluted paper cups are a must, and it is best to dip the balls in the caramelized sugar as close to serving time as possible.

**MAKES ABOUT 45
GOLF BALL–SIZE BALLS**

CRÈME BRÛLÉE:

2 cups heavy cream

½ moist, flexible vanilla
  bean

4 large egg yolks

6 tablespoons sugar

1 batch White Cake
  (page 34), baked, cooled,
  and crumbled

2 (12 x 3-inch) Styrofoam
  cake dummies (round or
  square)

45 (6-inch) lollipop sticks

3 cups sugar (see the Note)

⅔ cup light corn syrup (see
  the Note)

⅔ cup water (see the
  Note)

45 miniature fluted paper
  cups

1   To make the crème brûlée: Position a rack in the middle of the oven. Preheat the oven to 325°F. Place a 9½-inch tempered glass, deep-dish pie plate inside a large roasting pan; set aside.

2   Pour the cream into a small saucepan. Slit the vanilla bean in half lengthwise. Scrape the seeds into the cream and add the bean pieces to the pot as well. Bring to a boil over medium-high heat, taking care not to let it overflow, then turn off the heat and let the mixture steep for 15 minutes. Meanwhile, whisk together the egg yolks and sugar in a heatproof bowl until thick and creamy.

3   Rewarm the cream over medium heat; it should feel very warm to the touch. Slowly pour the warm cream into the egg mixture to temper the eggs, whisking constantly. Scrape any vanilla seeds into the egg mixture, as they might stick to the pan. Strain into the pie plate, discarding the bean halves. Fill the roasting pan with hot tap water to reach halfway up the sides of the pie plate.

4   Bake for 45 minutes, or just until the edges of the custard are set but the center still quivers if shaken gently. It will firm up upon cooling. Remove the pie plate from the roasting pan and let cool to room temperature on a wire rack. Refrigerate for at least 4 hours, or for up to 1 day covered with plastic wrap.

recipe continues

5 Combine the cake and about three-quarters of the chilled custard. Test by compressing and tasting, and add more custard only if needed for flavor and moisture. Roll into golf ball–size cake balls. Refrigerate until firm. This can be done 1 day ahead; store in an airtight container once they are firm. About 3 hours before proceeding, place the balls in the freezer.

6 Wrap the Styrofoam dummies with aluminum foil (to keep them clean for reuse). Remove the balls from the freezer. The balls will have a slightly flattened area from being stored, which is where you will insert a lollipop stick into each ball. Insert the sticks about halfway into the balls. Have a bowl filled with ice water next to the stove—the bowl must be large enough for you to plunge the bottom of a saucepan into it. Place the sugar, corn syrup, and water in a narrow, deep saucepan and stir to combine. Bring to a boil over medium-high heat, swirling the pan once or twice, but do not stir. Continue to boil until it reaches a deep golden color. Immediately plunge the bottom of the pot into the ice water and hold it in the water until any sputtering and/or boiling ceases.

7 Immediately place the saucepan on the work surface next to the Styrofoam dummies. Holding the end of a stick, insert a cake ball into the melted sugar, submerging the cake ball until the caramelized sugar touches the lollipop stick. Twirl the cake ball so that the cake is completely covered with caramel. (Do not drag it around the bowl, as the pull of the melted sugar might dislodge the stick.) Remove the cake ball from the caramelized sugar and let any excess drip off. This might take a few moments, so do not rush this step. Having finished cake balls that look neat and perfectly round largely depends on this step. Try holding the cake ball straight down and quickly rotating your hand in a circular motion to encourage centrifugal force to help excess sugar drip away. Once there is no extra caramelized sugar on the cake ball, insert the free end of the lollipop stick into the Styrofoam. (If you try to press it

in slowly, it might not go through the foil easily; you need to use a quick stabbing motion to get the job done. Alternatively, you can make holes with a sharp metal skewer first, then insert the lollipop sticks). Repeat until all the cake balls are coated. Allow the sugar to harden completely. This might take about 15 minutes at cool room temperature.

8   Arrange fluted paper cups side by side in a large, flat airtight container. Pick up a cake ball by the lollipop stick in one hand and with the other hand, place your index finger and thumb right at the juncture of the cake ball and the stick. Twist the stick very slowly and gently, or give it a wiggle side to side, and it should dislodge without cracking the sugar coating. Remove and discard the stick, and place the cake ball in a paper cup with the tiny hole left by the stick on the underside. Repeat with the remaining balls. Cover the container and serve within 2 hours.

Note: Caramelizing sugar can be tricky if you are not familiar with the process. If you cook the sugar mixture for too short a period of time, the color and flavor will be too light and weak. If you cook it for too long, it will be too dark and bitter. But do not fret, because there truly is a range of color and flavor that is not only appropriate but also delicious. If you do not have a lot of experience working with cooked sugar, I suggest making the caramelized sugar twice in succession, as it is easier to control smaller batches. Simply divide the sugar, corn syrup, and water amounts in half and use a clean pot for each batch.

The Crunchie-Munchie

If you are a fan of salty-sweet combinations, this is the perfect cake ball for you. The inside is moist milk chocolate brownie and milk chocolate ganache. Dip in your choice of chocolate (I use semisweet in the recipe) and then coat with a mixture of pretzels, potato chips, mini chocolate morsels, and caramel corn.

●　　●　　●

1　Combine the brownie and ½ cup of the ganache. Test by compressing and tasting, and add more ganache only if needed for flavor and moisture. Roll into golf ball–size cake balls. Refrigerate until firm. This can be done 1 day ahead; store in an airtight container once they are firm.

2　Line a rimmed baking sheet with parchment paper or aluminum foil. Toss the caramel corn, potato chips, pretzels, and mini morsels together in a bowl. Melt the chocolate in the microwave or a double boiler. Dip the balls one at a time in the chocolate, encouraging any excess chocolate to drip back into the container. Place, evenly spaced, on the prepared pans. Sprinkle a generous amount of the topping mixture on top of each cake ball while the chocolate is still wet. Use your fingers to scoop up additional topping and press to the sides of the balls. These balls look best when they are covered as completely as possible. Refrigerate briefly until the chocolate is set. Trim the bottoms, if needed. Place each cake ball in a paper cup, if desired. Place in a single layer in an airtight container and refrigerate for up to 4 days. Bring to room temperature before serving.

Note: **Since these cake balls are all about excess, why not divide the batch into thirds and dip some in dark, some in white, and some in milk chocolate?**

MAKES ABOUT 28 GOLF BALL–SIZE BALLS

1 batch Milk Chocolate Brownies (page 38), baked, cooled, and crumbled

½ batch Milk Chocolate Ganache (page 43), at room temperature, ready to use (should be soft and spreadable)

1 cup crushed caramel corn (about ½ inch around)

1 cup crushed potato chips (about ½ inch across)

1 cup crushed thin pretzel sticks (¼ to ½ inch long)

1 cup miniature semisweet chocolate morsels

1 pound semisweet chocolate, such as Callebaut or Ghirardelli, finely chopped

28 miniature fluted paper cups (optional)

Gingerbread
CAKE BALLS

This is a classic dark, spicy gingerbread. I used the basic version from *The Joy of Cooking* (Scribner, 1997) for inspiration, added some white pepper and unsulfured molasses, and tweaked the technique a tad. This gingerbread cake is so moist that it can be made into balls with no added binder. This is a nice change of pace when you want a not-too-sweet cake ball. It also works wonderfully with Cream Cheese Frosting, as presented here. You might be surprised at how superb the gingerbread flavor is with the dark chocolate coating; you will be a convert.

**MAKES ABOUT 40
GOLF BALL–SIZE BALLS**

1¾ cups all-purpose flour

1 tablespoon ground ginger

2 teaspoons ground cinnamon

1 teaspoon baking soda

¼ teaspoon ground cloves

¼ teaspoon ground white pepper

¼ teaspoon salt

½ cup (1 stick) unsalted butter, at room temperature, cut into small pieces

½ cup firmly packed light brown sugar

1 cup unsulfured molasses

1 large egg, at room temperature

½ cup boiling water

1 Position a rack in the middle of the oven. Preheat the oven to 350°F. Coat the inside of a 9-inch square pan with nonstick cooking spray; set aside.

2 Whisk together the flour, ginger, cinnamon, baking soda, cloves, white pepper, and salt in a medium bowl to aerate and combine; set aside.

3 With an electric mixer on medium-high speed, beat the butter until creamy, about 2 minutes. Gradually add the brown sugar and beat until very light and fluffy, about 3 minutes, scraping down the bowl once or twice. Beat in the molasses until combined, then beat in the egg until combined, again scraping down the bowl once or twice.

4 For the best cake texture, add the flour mixture all at once and beat briefly; there should still be white streaks. Then add the boiling water all at once and beat until the batter is combined and smooth. Pour the batter into the prepared pan.

5 Bake for about 25 minutes, or until a toothpick inserted in the center shows a few moist crumbs when removed. Let cool completely in the pan on a wire rack. The cake is ready to use. Alternatively, double-wrap the pan in plastic wrap and store at room temperature for up to 1 day before proceeding.

6 To make the cake balls, crumble the cooled cake and combine with ½ cup of the frosting. Test by compressing and tasting, and add more frosting only if needed for flavor and moisture. Roll into golf ball–size cake balls. Refrigerate until firm. This can be done 1 day ahead; store in an airtight container once they are firm.

7 Line two rimmed baking sheets with parchment paper or aluminum foil. Remove 3 balls and crumble them finely to use as decoration; set aside. (You can grate them on a box grater for a fine crumb.) Melt the chocolate in the microwave or a double boiler. Dip the balls one at a time in the chocolate, encouraging any excess chocolate to drip back into the container. Place, evenly spaced, on the prepared pans. Sprinkle a few gingerbread crumbs on top of each cake ball while the chocolate is still wet. Refrigerate briefly until the chocolate is set. Trim the bottoms, if needed. Place each cake ball in a paper cup, if desired. Place in a single layer in an airtight container and refrigerate for up to 4 days. Bring to room temperature before serving.

½ batch Cream Cheese Frosting (page 40), ready to use

1¼ pounds semisweet chocolate, such as Callebaut or Ghirardelli, finely chopped

40 miniature fluted paper cups (optional)

Disco

CAKE BALLS

These are very colorful and sparkly, hence the name. This is all about the decoration, which is provided by colored sugar and/or edible glitter. You can use several different colors, or multi-colored or even metallic options. I like using superfine sugar or Disco Dust. You could also go thematic: reds and greens for Christmas; Mom's favorite colors for Mother's Day; the birthday girl or boy's favorite colors—you get the idea. This is a great project to make with kids during school holidays or as a birthday party project for all the guests. Adults will want to pitch in too with this fun, crafty recipe.

**MAKES ABOUT 52
GOLF BALL–SIZE BALLS**

1 batch White Cake (page 34), baked, cooled, and crumbled

1 batch Confectioners' Sugar Frosting (page 39), ready to use

1²/₃ pounds white chocolate, such as Callebaut or Valrhona Ivoire, finely chopped

Assorted colored sugars and edible glitter

52 miniature fluted paper cups (optional)

1   Combine the cake and about 1 cup of the frosting. Test by compressing and tasting, and add more frosting only if needed for flavor and moisture. Roll into golf ball–size cake balls. Refrigerate until firm. This can be done 1 day ahead; store in an airtight container once firm.

2   Line two rimmed baking sheets with parchment paper or aluminum foil. Melt the chocolate in the microwave or a double boiler. Dip the balls one at a time in the chocolate, encouraging any excess chocolate to drip back into the container. Place, evenly spaced, on the prepared pans. Sprinkle a generous amount of colored sugar or edible glitter on top of each cake ball while the chocolate is still wet. If you want to coat the balls all the way around, place the colored sugar or glitter of choice in a small bowl. Be sure all excess chocolate has dripped off, then drop one ball at a time into the bowl and move the bowl in a circular motion to encourage the ball to rotate completely within the decorative coating. Use a fork to scoop up and remove the ball from the mixture and place on the pan. Refrigerate briefly until the chocolate is set. Trim the bottoms, if needed. Place each cake ball in a paper cup, if desired. Place in a single layer in an airtight container and refrigerate for up to 3 days. Bring to room temperature before serving.

Note: **The cake and frosting suggested here is just that—a mere suggestion. Take note, however, that the colors of the decorations will look best on white chocolate–dipped cake balls.**

Espresso Brownie

CAKE BALLS

For coffee lovers only! These pack not only a serious espresso flavor but also quite
a caffeine punch. The espresso brownie is so moist that it doesn't need any binder.
Rolled into balls, dipped in a dark chocolate shell, and topped with crumbled
chocolate-covered coffee beans, these are the most robust cake balls in the book.
I recommend a smaller size for these cake balls, as they are dense and rich, with a
brownie-like texture.

**MAKES ABOUT 60
1-INCH BALLS**

1 cup all-purpose flour

3/4 teaspoon baking powder

1/4 teaspoon salt

3/4 cup (1 1/2 sticks) unsalted
butter, melted

3/4 cup granulated sugar

3/4 cup firmly packed light
brown sugar

1 teaspoon pure vanilla
extract

1/4 cup instant espresso
powder

3 large eggs, at room
temperature

1   Position a rack in the middle of the oven. Preheat the oven to
350°F. Coat the inside of a 9-inch square pan with nonstick cooking
spray; set aside.

2   Whisk the flour, baking powder, and salt in a small bowl to aerate
and combine.

3   Whisk together the melted butter, sugars, and vanilla. Whisk in the
espresso powder, then add the eggs one at a time, whisking well after
each addition until smooth. Add the flour mixture, stirring until just
combined. Scrape into the prepared pan.

4   Bake for about 40 minutes, or until a toothpick inserted in the
center comes out with some moist crumbs clinging. Let cool completely
in the pan on a wire rack. The brownie is ready to use. Alternatively,
double-wrap the pan in plastic wrap and store at room temperature for
up to 1 day before proceeding.

5   To make the cake balls, crumble the cooled brownie and work
with your hands (or the flat paddle of an electric mixer) until the
crumbs come together. Roll into 1-inch cake balls. Refrigerate until firm,
if needed.

●　●　●　●　●　●　●　●　●　●

6　Line a rimmed baking sheet with parchment paper or aluminum foil. Crush the chocolate-covered espresso beans. You can use the flat bottom of a heavy pan or place them in a zipper-top bag and crush with a rolling pin. Melt the chocolate in the microwave or a double boiler. Dip the balls one at a time in the chocolate, encouraging any excess chocolate to drip back into the container. Place, evenly spaced, on the prepared pan. Sprinkle some crushed espresso beans on top of each cake ball while the chocolate is still wet. Refrigerate briefly until the chocolate is set. Trim the bottoms, if needed. Place each cake ball in a paper cup, if desired. Place in a single layer in an airtight container and refrigerate for up to 3 days. Bring to room temperature before serving.

1/3 cup chocolate-covered espresso beans

1 pound semisweet chocolate, such as Callebaut or Valrhona Equatoriale, finely chopped

60 (1-inch) fluted paper cups (optional)

Dulce de Leche

CAKE BALLS

If you like caramel and burnt sugar flavors, this recipe will tickle your taste buds. Dulce de leche is sweetened condensed milk that has been cooked down until the sugar has caramelized, yielding a thick, sticky, caramel-flavored milk with a creamy, spreadable texture. While it can be made at home, it can also be purchased. I use Nestlé brand, which can often be found in the Spanish foods section in the supermarket. The dulce de leche is combined with yellow cake, dipped in milk chocolate, and drizzled with caramel, and the result will appeal to kids and adults alike.

1   Combine the cake with ¾ cup of the dulce de leche. Test by compressing and tasting, and add more dulce de leche only if needed for flavor and moisture. Roll into golf ball–size cake balls. Refrigerate until firm. This can be done 1 day ahead; store in an airtight container once they are firm.

2   Line two rimmed baking sheets with parchment paper or aluminum foil. Melt the chocolate in the microwave or a double boiler. Dip the balls one at a time in the chocolate, encouraging any excess chocolate to drip back into the container. Place, evenly spaced, on the prepared pans. Refrigerate briefly until the chocolate is set.

3   Melt the caramel in the microwave until fluid, watching carefully so that it doesn't boil. Use a fork to drizzle caramel zigzags on top of each ball. Refrigerate again until the caramel is set. Trim the bottoms, if needed. Place each cake ball in a paper cup, if desired. Place in a single layer in an airtight container and refrigerate for up to 4 days. Bring to room temperature before serving.

Note: Block caramel, especially Nestlé brand, is available from several baking supply sources and has a far superior taste to the smaller individual caramels that you might find at the supermarket. It is well worth seeking out. See Resources (page 164).

MAKES ABOUT 56 GOLF BALL–SIZE BALLS

- 1 batch Yellow Buttermilk Cake (page 29), baked, cooled, and crumbled
- 1 (13.4-ounce) can dulce de leche
- 1¾ pounds milk chocolate, such as Callebaut or Valrhona Jivara, finely chopped
- 5 ounces caramel, such as Nestlé (see the Note)
- 56 miniature fluted paper cups (optional)

Fudgy Brownie Nut

CAKE BALLS

These are dark and chocolaty and punctuated with walnuts or pecans. The chocolate flavor is so rich that I think that you need the nuts to add interest and cut the richness. These keep very well and will please those who like dark chocolate. Dense and delicious, there is nothing delicate about them.

**MAKES ABOUT 22
GOLF BALL-SIZE BALLS**

1 batch Fudgy Brownies (page 37), made with nuts, baked, cooled, and crumbled

2/3 pound semisweet chocolate, such as Callebaut or Ghirardelli, finely chopped

22 miniature fluted paper cups (optional)

1   Roll the crumbled brownie into golf ball–size balls. You might find a squeezing action is needed with this hefty cake ball in order to form it into rounds. Refrigerate briefly while you melt the chocolate and prepare the pan. This can be done 1 day ahead; store in an airtight container.

2   Line a rimmed baking sheet with parchment paper or aluminum foil. Melt the chocolate in the microwave or a double boiler, and remove and reserve about ¼ cup. Dip the balls one at a time in the larger quantity of chocolate, encouraging any excess chocolate to drip back into the container. Place, evenly spaced, on the prepared pan. Refrigerate briefly until the chocolate is set.

3   Place the reserved melted chocolate in a parchment cone (see page 25). Snip a small opening in the cone's tip and pipe zigzags over the tops of the balls. Refrigerate again until the chocolate is set. Trim the bottoms, if needed. Place each cake ball in a paper cup, if desired. Place in a single layer in an airtight container and refrigerate for up to 5 days. Bring to room temperature before serving.

Jam-Filled

CAKE BALLS

Any basic cake, such as yellow, white, or chocolate, can be moistened with jam to make a very flavorful, fruity, easy cake ball. Note that the "jams" I use are sugar-free fruit spreads. These are jam-like spreads typically sweetened with fruit juice instead of sugar and will be labeled as such. (They are not the ones that use artificial sweeteners, which I do not recommend.) The 100 percent fruit spreads have a very concentrated fruit flavor and are not as sweet as typical sugar-sweetened jams, which is a boon all the way around. I particularly like the raspberry, strawberry, and apricot flavors.

● ● ●

1 Combine the cake and about ¾ cup of the fruit spread. Test by compressing, and add as much of the remaining fruit spread as the cake will hold. Roll into golf ball–size cake balls. Refrigerate until firm. This can be done 1 day ahead; store in an airtight container once they are firm.

2 Line two rimmed baking sheets with parchment paper or aluminum foil. Melt the chocolate in the microwave or a double boiler. Dip the balls one at a time in the chocolate, encouraging any excess chocolate to drip back into the container. Place, evenly spaced, on the prepared pans. Refrigerate briefly until the chocolate is set. Trim the bottoms, if needed. Place each cake ball in a paper cup, if desired. Place in a single layer in an airtight container and refrigerate for up to 3 days. Bring to room temperature before serving.

Note: **You can decorate the cake balls to go along with the flavor of jam used, such as using a bit of dried apricot on top when using apricot spread or a sprinkle of red edible glitter or sprinkles or crushed dehydrated fruit for the raspberry or strawberry spreads. See Resources (page 164) for Just Tomatoes, Etc.! brand freeze-dried fruit.**

MAKES 50 TO 60
GOLF BALL–SIZE BALLS,
DEPENDING ON CAKE USED

1 batch Super-Easy Yellow Cake (page 30), Super-Easy Chocolate Cake (page 31), or White Cake (page 34), baked, cooled, and crumbled

1¼ cups 100% fruit spread, such as raspberry, strawberry, or apricot

2 pounds Callebaut semisweet, white, or milk chocolate, or Ghirardelli semisweet or milk chocolate, finely chopped

60 miniature fluted paper cups (optional)

Peppermint–White Chocolate

CAKE BALLS

If you like chocolate and mint, you have two choices within this book. For a dark chocolate and mint combo, turn to page 49 for the After-Dinner Chocolate-Mint Cake Balls. This cake ball recipe features white chocolate and red and white peppermint candy. You can adjust the strength of the mint filling easily by adding more or less of the peppermint flavoring.

● ● ●

**MAKES ABOUT 48
GOLF BALL–SIZE BALLS**

½ teaspoon peppermint flavoring, such as Boyajian, or to taste

1 batch White Chocolate Ganache (page 43), ready to use (should be soft and spreadable)

1 batch White Cake (page 34), baked, cooled, and crumbled

1½ pounds white chocolate, such as Callebaut or Valrhona Ivoire, finely chopped

½ cup finely crushed red and white peppermint candy

48 miniature fluted paper cups (optional)

1   Stir the peppermint flavoring into the ganache. Combine the cake and 1 cup of the ganache. Test by compressing and tasting, and add more ganache only if needed for flavor and moisture. Roll into golf ball–size cake balls. Refrigerate until firm. This can be done 1 day ahead; store in an airtight container once they are firm.

2   Line two rimmed baking sheets with parchment paper or aluminum foil. Melt the chocolate in the microwave or a double boiler. Dip the balls one at a time in the chocolate, encouraging any excess chocolate to drip back into the container. Place, evenly spaced, on the prepared pans. Sprinkle a bit of crushed candy on top of each cake ball while the chocolate is still wet. Refrigerate briefly until the chocolate is set. Trim the bottoms, if needed. Place each cake ball in a paper cup, if desired. Place in a single layer in an airtight container and refrigerate for up to 4 days. Bring to room temperature before serving.

German Chocolate

CAKE BALLS

All the classic flavors and textures of German chocolate cake are in this cake ball: coconut, chocolate, and pecans. The traditional frosting for that cake is cooked on top of the stove and is uniquely sticky, chewy, and sweet; here it is folded into chocolate cake to make these balls. Dipped in a dark chocolate shell, these are then further embellished with a generous shower of more coconut and pecans. For the photo, we used larger shaved coconut pieces on the exterior of the cake ball for an elegant look, but sweetened long-shred coconut works just as well.

1   To make the frosting: Place the evaporated milk and sugar in a large saucepan and whisk to combine. Whisk in the egg yolks and butter pieces. Gently cook over medium heat until the mixture reaches a simmer, and then cook for 6 to 7 minutes, whisking frequently, until it thickens and darkens slightly. Remove from the heat and stir in the vanilla, coconut, and pecans. Cool, stirring occasionally to release heat, until just warm to the touch and thickened. Let cool completely at room temperature.

2   Combine the cake and about 2 cups of the frosting (the recipe yields about 2½ cups). Test by compressing and tasting, and add more frosting only if needed for flavor and moisture. Roll into golf ball–size cake balls. Refrigerate until firm. This can be done 1 day ahead; store in an airtight container once they are firm.

recipe continues

MAKES ABOUT 64 GOLF BALL–SIZE BALLS

FROSTING:

Scant 1 cup evaporated milk

Scant 1 cup sugar

3 large egg yolks

7½ tablespoons unsalted butter, at room temperature, cut into pieces

1 teaspoon pure vanilla extract

1½ cups sweetened long-shred coconut

Scant 1 cup toasted pecan halves, chopped

1 batch Super-Easy
  Chocolate Cake
  (page 31), baked, cooled,
  and crumbled

1 cup sweetened long-
  shred coconut or shaved
  coconut (sweetened or
  unsweetened)

1 cup toasted pecan halves,
  finely chopped

2 pounds semisweet
  chocolate, such as
  Callebaut or Ghirardelli,
  finely chopped

64 miniature fluted paper
  cups (optional)

3 Line two rimmed baking sheets with parchment paper or aluminum foil. Toss together the coconut and pecans in a small bowl. Melt the chocolate in the microwave or a double boiler. Dip the balls one at a time in the chocolate, encouraging any excess chocolate to drip back into the container. Place, evenly spaced, on the prepared pans. Sprinkle a generous amount of the coconut-pecan mixture on top of each cake ball while the chocolate is still wet. Refrigerate briefly until the chocolate is set. Trim the bottoms, if needed. Place each cake ball in a paper cup, if desired. Place in a single layer in an airtight container and refrigerate for up to 4 days. Bring to room temperature before serving.

Key Lime
CAKE BALLS

People frequently ask me how I develop recipes. In this instance, the Zesty Lemon Cake Balls (page 138) were already a fave among my tasters, and one day I wondered what a lime version would taste like. Key lime pie popped into my head, and this cake ball was born. The balls are dipped in white chocolate, and a sprinkle of graham crackers crowns the top. By the way, you can use regular (Persian) limes; they are tarter than Key limes, and I happen to prefer them.

1   To make the filling: Whisk together the sweetened condensed milk, lime juice, and egg yolks in a small saucepan and cook over medium heat, whisking often, until thickened, about 10 minutes. The mixture should barely simmer around the edges of the pot and should be thick enough to see whisk marks. Let cool. It is ready to use, or it may be refrigerated in an airtight container overnight.

2   Crumble the cooled cake and combine with three-quarters of the lime filling. Test by compressing and tasting, and add more lime filling only if needed for flavor and moisture. Roll into golf ball–size cake balls. Refrigerate until firm. This can be done 1 day ahead; store in an airtight container once they are firm.

3   Line two rimmed baking sheets with parchment paper or aluminum foil. Melt the chocolate in the microwave or a double boiler. Dip the balls one at a time in the chocolate, encouraging any excess chocolate to drip back into the container. Place, evenly spaced, on the prepared pans. Sprinkle a bit of graham cracker crumbs on top of each cake ball while the chocolate is still wet. Refrigerate briefly until the chocolate is set. Trim the bottoms, if needed. Place each cake ball in a paper cup, if desired. Place in a single layer in an airtight container and refrigerate for up to 3 days. Bring to room temperature before serving.

Note: You can add a drop or two of green food coloring to the filling once you have removed it from the heat, if you like.

MAKES ABOUT 52 GOLF BALL–SIZE BALLS

LIME FILLING:

1 (14-ounce) can sweetened condensed milk

½ cup freshly squeezed lime juice

4 large egg yolks

1 batch White Cake (page 34), made with 1 tablespoon freshly grated lime zest added along with the vanilla extract

1²/3 pounds white chocolate, such as Callebaut or Valrhona Ivoire, finely chopped

½ cup graham cracker crumbs

52 miniature fluted paper cups (optional)

Marbleized Black and White

BROWNIE BALLS

The basic Fudgy Brownie recipe makes a dense, rich brownie. Here I recommend that you leave out the nuts when making the base, but add white chocolate morsels while you are forming the balls; the cake balls will be black and white inside. Continuing the color theme, the outer coating is a marbleized combination of semisweet and white chocolates. Note the chocolates that are recommended; these chocolates are very fluid when melted, which is necessary for the marbleizing technique.

**MAKES ABOUT 22
GOLF BALL–SIZE BALLS**

1 batch Fudgy Brownies (page 37), made without nuts, baked, cooled, and crumbled

2/3 cup (about 4 ounces) white chocolate morsels, chopped

10 ounces semisweet chocolate, such as Callebaut or Valrhona Equatoriale, finely chopped

6 ounces white chocolate, such as Callebaut or Valrhona Ivoire, finely chopped

22 miniature fluted paper cups (optional)

1   Combine the crumbled brownie with the chopped white chocolate morsels. You have to be firm and use your hands for the best results. You might find a squeezing action is needed with this hefty cake ball in order to form it into rounds. Roll into golf ball–size cake balls. Refrigerate until firm. This can be done 1 day ahead; store in an airtight container once they are firm.

2   Line a rimmed baking sheet with parchment paper or aluminum foil. Melt the chocolates separately in the microwave or double boilers. Pour about one-quarter of the semisweet chocolate into a small bowl. Pour about one-quarter of the white chocolate on top of the semisweet chocolate in a swirl pattern. Dip the balls one at a time, submerging them and turning them over carefully so that swirls of both white and dark chocolate cover each ball, encouraging any excess chocolate to drip back into the container. Place, evenly spaced, on the prepared pans. Create new batches of white and dark chocolate as you go (with a clean bowl each time) to keep the "black and white" swirling pattern distinct (it will get muddy after five or so dips). Refrigerate briefly until the chocolate is set. Trim the bottoms, if needed. Place each cake ball in a paper cup, if desired. Place in a single layer in an airtight container and refrigerate for up to 4 days. Bring to room temperature before serving.

Note: You could try this marbleizing technique with Wilton Candy Melts, if you like. You can take advantage of any of the colors available; just make sure the colors are very distinct from one another.

Milk Chocolate Bacon Bourbon

CAKE BALLS

Bacon has found its footing in desserts recently, particularly when paired with chocolate. It seems to be part of the salty-sweet craze and works quite nicely with a hit of bourbon when combined with chocolate cake and a milk chocolate ganache. I used Four Roses Single Barrel bourbon while developing the recipe. Its long finish was perfect when blended with the other two primary flavors. This one is for the adventurous.

**MAKES ABOUT 56
GOLF BALL-SIZE BALLS**

12 slices meaty bacon

1 batch Super-Easy Chocolate Cake (page 31), baked, cooled, and crumbled

¼ cup bourbon

½ batch Milk Chocolate Ganache (page 43), at room temperature, ready to use (should be soft and spreadable)

1¾ pounds milk chocolate, such as Callebaut or Valrhona Jivara, finely chopped

Coarse salt, for sprinkling (see the Note)

56 miniature fluted paper cups (optional)

1   Cook the bacon until crisp and drain on paper towels to remove excess fat. Let cool completely, then crumble into very small pieces.

2   Place the crumbled cake in a wide bowl (the more surface area, the better). Drizzle some of the bourbon over the cake crumbs, tossing the cake as you go. Your aim is to distribute the liquid as evenly as possible. Keep pouring and tossing until all of the liquid is absorbed. Toss in the bacon pieces, then add ¾ cup of the ganache. Test by compressing and tasting, and add more ganache only if needed for flavor and moisture. Roll into golf ball–size cake balls. Refrigerate until firm. This can be done 1 day ahead; store in an airtight container once they are firm.

3   Line two rimmed baking sheets with parchment paper or aluminum foil. Melt the chocolate in the microwave or a double boiler. Dip the balls one at a time in the chocolate, encouraging any excess chocolate to drip back into the container. Place, evenly spaced, on the prepared pans. Sprinkle a few grains of salt on top of each cake ball while the chocolate is still wet. Refrigerate briefly until the chocolate is set. Trim the bottoms, if needed. Place each cake ball in a paper cup, if desired. Place in a single layer in an airtight container and refrigerate for up to 3 days. Bring to room temperature before serving.

Note: There is a specialty product called Bacon Salt made by J&D Foods (see Resources, page 164) that is, believe it or not, fat free, kosher, and vegetarian—and yet tastes like bacon! It is great used instead of the coarse salt for the top of these cake balls.

Mudslide

CAKE BALLS

I took a poll of what popular alcoholic drink I should turn into a cake ball and the answer was clear: the Mudslide. This potent beverage combines equal portions of vodka, Kahlúa coffee liqueur, and Baileys Irish Cream liqueur. Here the vodka is left out, as it does not add any flavor. Kahlúa and Baileys are combined with yellow cake and dipped in either milk or dark chocolate. These cake balls must be frozen before coating; this helps them hold together during dipping. A food disher or ice cream scoop is very helpful with this recipe during the ball-forming stage.

1   Combine the sugar and water in a small saucepan and stir to combine. Bring to a boil over medium-high heat, swirling the pan once or twice to encourage the sugar to dissolve. Boil for 30 seconds to 1 minute, or until the sugar is dissolved. Let cool and then stir in both liqueurs. Transfer to a large measuring cup or other container with a spout.

2   Have the crumbled cake in a wide bowl (the more surface area, the better). Drizzle some of the alcohol mixture over the cake crumbs, tossing the cake as you go. Your aim is to distribute the liquid as evenly as possible. Keep pouring and tossing until all of the liquid is absorbed. Now use your hands to thoroughly mix the cake and liqueur. Roll into golf ball–size cake balls. Freeze until firm. This can be done 1 day ahead; store in an airtight container once they are firm.

3   Line two rimmed baking sheets with parchment paper or aluminum foil. Melt the chocolate in the microwave or a double boiler. Dip the balls one at a time in the chocolate, encouraging any excess chocolate to drip back into the container. Place, evenly spaced, on the prepared pans. Refrigerate briefly until the chocolate is set. Trim the bottoms, if needed. Place each cake ball in a paper cup, if desired. Place in a single layer in an airtight container and refrigerate for up to 4 days. Bring to room temperature before serving.

MAKES ABOUT 52 GOLF BALL–SIZE BALLS

1 cup sugar

¼ cup water

½ cup Baileys Irish Cream

½ cup Kahlúa

1 batch Yellow Buttermilk Cake (page 29), baked, cooled, and crumbled

1²⁄₃ pounds semisweet or milk chocolate, such as Callebaut, Valrhona, or Scharffen Berger, finely chopped

52 miniature fluted paper cups (optional)

Mocha Toffee Crunch

CAKE BALLS

I love the combination of chocolate, coffee, and toffee, and they are brought together in this crunchy cake ball. Chocolate cake is combined with a mocha frosting and dipped in toffee chip–studded milk chocolate. Fabulous.

1   Dissolve the instant espresso powder in the vanilla in a small bowl and then beat the mixture into the frosting. Crumble the cake in a large bowl and combine with about 1 cup of the frosting. Test by compressing and tasting, and add more frosting only if needed for flavor and moisture. Roll into golf ball–size cake balls. Refrigerate until firm. This can be done 1 day ahead; store in an airtight container once they are firm.

2   Line two rimmed baking sheets with parchment paper or aluminum foil. Melt the chocolate in the microwave or a double boiler; stir in 1¾ cups of the toffee bits. Dip the balls one at a time in this chocolate-toffee mixture, encouraging any excess chocolate to drip back into the container, and place, evenly spaced, on the prepared pans. Sprinkle a few of the remaining toffee bits on top of each cake ball while the chocolate is still wet. Refrigerate briefly until the chocolate is set. Trim the bottoms, if necessary. Place each cake ball in a paper cup, if desired. Place in a single layer in an airtight container and refrigerate for up to 4 days. Bring to room temperature before serving.

Note: **These also work well with semisweet chocolate as an outer coating.**

MAKES ABOUT 60 GOLF BALL–SIZE BALLS

- 1½ teaspoons instant espresso powder
- 1 teaspoon pure vanilla extract
- 1 batch Fudgy Chocolate Frosting (page 41), ready to use
- 1 batch Super-Easy Chocolate Cake (page 31), made with 2 teaspoons instant espresso powder dissolved into the vanilla extract
- 2 pounds milk chocolate, such as Callebaut or Valrhona Jivara, finely chopped
- 2 cups toffee bits, such as Heath Bits 'O Brickle
- 60 miniature fluted paper cups (optional)

Nutella Cake Balls

WITH CARAMELIZED HAZELNUTS

Nutella has a cult-like following. It is a creamy milk chocolate–hazelnut spread that, thankfully, can be found in most supermarkets alongside the peanut butter. Fans eat it by the spoonful (or smeared on a banana, as I do), but here it is used in an elegant cake ball that will appeal to both kids and adults. White cake is combined with Nutella, rolled into balls, and dipped in milk chocolate gianduja, which is a bar chocolate also made from milk chocolate and hazelnuts. Crunchy caramelized hazelnuts are sprinkled on top; they can be made ahead.

MAKES ABOUT 54 GOLF BALL–SIZE BALLS

CARAMELIZED HAZELNUTS:

1/2 cup sugar

1 tablespoon plus 2 teaspoons water

2/3 cup skinned hazelnuts, chopped (see the Notes)

1 batch White Cake (page 34), baked, cooled, and crumbled

1½ cups Nutella, at room temperature

1²/3 pounds milk chocolate gianduja, such as Callebaut, finely chopped

54 miniature fluted paper cups (optional)

1   To make the caramelized hazelnuts: Line a rimmed baking sheet with parchment paper or aluminum foil. Stir the sugar and water together in a small saucepan. Bring to a simmer over medium-high heat, swirling the pan once or twice, but do not stir. Cook until the sugar is caramelized and has turned a medium golden brown. Stir in the hazelnuts until coated, then immediately scrape out onto the prepared pan. Allow to cool; the caramelized sugar will harden. Break off pieces of nut brittle, place on a cutting board, and use a large chef's knife to chop it finely; set aside. This can be done up to 4 days ahead; store in an airtight container at room temperature.

2   Combine the cake and 1 cup of the Nutella. The mixture will be very sticky; if you have an electric mixer and paddle attachment, use them to help combine the cake and Nutella. Otherwise, get in there with your hands. You might find a squeezing action is needed in order to uniformly incorporate the Nutella. Test by compressing and tasting, and add more Nutella only if needed for flavor and moisture. Roll into golf ball–size cake balls. Refrigerate until firm. This can be done 1 day ahead; store in an airtight container once they are firm.

recipe continues

3 Line two rimmed baking sheets with parchment paper or aluminum foil. Melt the gianduja in the microwave or a double boiler. Dip the balls one at a time in the gianduja, encouraging any excess chocolate to drip back into the container. Place, evenly spaced, on the prepared pans. Sprinkle a bit of the caramelized nuts on top of each cake ball while the gianduja is still wet. Trim the bottoms, if needed. Refrigerate briefly until the gianduja is set. Place each cake ball in a paper cup, if desired. Place in a single layer in an airtight container and refrigerate for up to 4 days. Bring to room temperature before serving.

Notes: **To skin the hazelnuts, place in a single layer on a rimmed baking sheet and bake at 350°F until the skins have split and the nuts are golden brown. Let cool, then vigorously rub the nuts between clean kitchen towels to remove the skins.**

If you know that you will be serving these cake balls to an adults-only crowd, sprinkle the cake crumbs with some Frangelico hazelnut liqueur before folding in the Nutella.

The gianduja can be found at some specialty shops and through mail-order (see Resources, page 164).

Peanut Butter–Milk Chocolate

CAKE BALLS

These are like a Reese's peanut butter cup in cake ball form. Yellow or white cake is combined with peanut butter for a moist, nutty interior. The ball gets dipped in milk chocolate, of course, just like the candy. Decorate the top with a squiggle of milk chocolate or a few crushed peanuts.

1   Combine the cake and 1¼ cups of the peanut butter. The mixture will be very sticky; if you have an electric mixer and paddle attachment, use them to help combine the cake and peanut butter. Otherwise, get in there with your hands. You might find a squeezing action is needed in order to uniformly incorporate the peanut butter. Test by compressing and tasting, and add more peanut butter only if needed for flavor and moisture. Roll into golf ball–size cake balls. Refrigerate until firm. This can be done 1 day ahead; store in an airtight container once they are firm.

2   Line two rimmed baking sheets with parchment paper or aluminum foil. Melt the chocolate in the microwave or a double boiler. Remove and reserve about ¼ cup of melted chocolate. Dip the balls one at a time in the larger amount of chocolate, encouraging any excess chocolate to drip back into the container. Place, evenly spaced, on the prepared pans.

3   Place the reserved melted chocolate in a parchment cone (see page 25), snip a small opening from the tip, and pipe a design of your choice on top of each ball, if desired. Alternatively, sprinkle the wet cake balls with a bit of chopped peanuts. Refrigerate briefly until the chocolate is set. Trim the bottoms, if needed. Place each cake ball in a paper cup, if desired. Place in a single layer in an airtight container and refrigerate for up to 3 days. Bring to room temperature before serving.

MAKES ABOUT 65 GOLF BALL–SIZE BALLS

1 batch Super-Easy Yellow Cake (page 30) or White Cake (page 34), baked, cooled, and crumbled

2 cups creamy peanut butter, such as Skippy, Jif, or Peter Pan (do not use natural peanut butter)

2⅛ pounds milk chocolate, such as Callebaut or Ghirardelli, finely chopped

½ cup finely chopped, lightly salted dry-roasted peanuts (optional)

65 miniature fluted paper cups (optional)

Oreo

CAKE BALLS

If you search the Internet for "Oreo Cake Balls," you will come up with many recipes and photographs. They are extremely popular because they are both tasty and ridiculously easy to make, but unfortunately most of the recipes are very skeletal and say things like use "one package cookies" and "one bar of chocolate bark"—hardly specific enough directions to help you be successful. Here is my version, with exact amounts and directions. Note that I have given you a cookie count, as there are many different size packages provided by Nabisco; even if they were to discontinue a particular size package, you would know how many cookies you need.

1   Place the cookies in the bowl of a food processor fitted with the metal blade and pulse on and off until they are reduced to large chunks; then let the machine run until the cookies are ground to very fine crumbs. Add the cream cheese and pulse on and off to begin combining the mixture, then let the machine run until the cookies and cream cheese are evenly combined. Roll the mixture into golf ball–size balls and refrigerate until firm. This can be done 1 day ahead; store in an airtight container once they are firm.

2   Line a rimmed baking sheet with parchment paper or aluminum foil. Melt the semisweet chocolate in the microwave or a double boiler. Dip the balls one at a time in the chocolate, encouraging any excess chocolate to drip back into the container. Place, evenly spaced, on the prepared pans.

3   Melt the white chocolate and place in a parchment cone (see page 25). Snip a small opening from the tip of the cone and pipe one stripe of white chocolate across each ball (to mimic the white filling of an Oreo). Refrigerate briefly until the chocolate is set. Trim the bottoms, if needed. Place each cake ball in a paper cup, if desired. Place in a single layer in an airtight container and refrigerate for up to 5 days. Bring to room temperature before serving.

**MAKES ABOUT 25
GOLF BALL–SIZE BALLS**

45 to 48 Oreo sandwich cookies (about a 1-pound package)

8 ounces full-fat cream cheese, cold, cut into pieces

13 ounces semisweet chocolate, such as Callebaut or Ghirardelli, finely chopped

3 ounces white chocolate, such as Callebaut, finely chopped

25 miniature fluted paper cups (optional)

Piña Colada

CAKE BALLS

The flavors of the drink—pineapple, coconut, and rum—are rolled up here into a neat little treat. The rum presence is subtle, but you should still consider this to be an adult cake ball. I like these balls dipped in any of the chocolates—white, milk, or semisweet.

MAKES ABOUT 72 GOLF BALL–SIZE BALLS

2 (14-ounce) cans pure unsweetened coconut milk

FILLING:

2 (8.25-ounce) cans crushed pineapple, with juice

1⅓ cups sugar

¼ cup gold rum

6 tablespoons cornstarch

1 batch Yellow Buttermilk Cake (page 29), made with 1¼ cups reduced coconut milk (from above) instead of buttermilk

½ cup gold rum

1   Pour both cans of coconut milk into a wide saucepan and bring to a simmer over medium heat (you might need a splatter shield). Simmer until reduced by half, 5 to 10 minutes; it should be visibly thickened. Let cool completely. You may refrigerate in an airtight container for up to 3 days. Bring to room temperature before proceeding.

2   To make the filling: Drain the pineapple, reserving the juice. Measure the liquid and remove and discard ¼ cup of juice. Stir together the sugar, pineapple with any remaining juice, rum, and cornstarch in a saucepan and bring to a boil over medium heat. Boil, stirring frequently, until thick and glossy. This will take at least 5 minutes, if not more. Let cool completely. You may refrigerate in an airtight container for up to 3 days. Bring to room temperature before proceeding.

3   Crumble the cooled cake and sprinkle the rum over the cake to distribute evenly. Add 1¼ cups of the pineapple filling. Test by compressing and tasting, and add more pineapple filling only if needed for flavor and moisture. Roll into golf ball–size cake balls. Refrigerate until firm. This can be done 1 day ahead; store in an airtight container once they are firm.

4 Line two rimmed baking sheets with parchment paper or aluminum foil. Melt the chocolate in the microwave or a double boiler. Dip the balls one at a time in the chocolate, encouraging any excess chocolate to drip back into the container. Place, evenly spaced, on the prepared pans. Sprinkle a bit of toasted coconut on top of each cake ball while the chocolate is still wet. Refrigerate briefly until the chocolate is set. Trim the bottoms, if needed. Place each cake ball in a paper cup, if desired. Place in a single layer in an airtight container and refrigerate for up to 3 days. Bring to room temperature before serving.

Note: Of course, you can dip some balls in white chocolate, some in milk chocolate, and some in semisweet, if desired. To make Pineapple-Coconut Cake Balls (without the alcohol), simply cook the filling with no rum and instead use the entire can of pineapple, juice and all. Don't sprinkle rum over the crumbled cake, either.

2¼ pounds white, milk, or dark chocolate, such as Callebaut or Valrhona, finely chopped

1 cup sweetened long-shred coconut, toasted and coarsely chopped

72 miniature fluted paper cups (optional)

Five Chocolates

CAKE BALLS

This is a cake ball where more is more—and more is great. Cocoa, dark chocolate, milk chocolate, white chocolate, and ganache are all combined in one cake ball. Use the best chocolates for the best results (see my specific recommendations).

MAKES ABOUT 64 GOLF BALL–SIZE BALLS

- 1 batch Super-Easy Chocolate Cake (page 31), baked, cooled, and crumbled
- 1 batch Dark Chocolate Ganache (page 42), made with Valrhona Equatoriale or other 55% chocolate, at room temperature, ready to use (should be soft and spreadable)
- 2¼ pounds bittersweet or semisweet chocolate, such as Valrhona Guanaja, Caraïbe, or Equatoriale, finely chopped
- 4 ounces milk chocolate, such as Callebaut or Valrhona Jivara, melted
- 4 ounces white chocolate, such as Callebaut or Valrhona Ivoire, melted
- 1 cup miniature semisweet chocolate morsels
- 64 miniature fluted paper cups (optional)

1 Combine the cake and about 1½ cups of the ganache. Test by compressing, and add as much of the remaining ganache as the cake will hold. Roll into golf ball–size cake balls. Refrigerate until firm. This can be done 1 day ahead; store in an airtight container once they are firm.

2 Line two rimmed baking sheets with parchment paper or aluminum foil. Melt the dark chocolate in the microwave or double boiler. Remove and reserve ¼ cup. Dip the balls one at a time in the larger amount of chocolate, encouraging any excess chocolate to drip back into the container. Place, evenly spaced, on the prepared pans. Refrigerate briefly until the chocolate is set. Trim the bottoms, if needed.

3 Place the melted milk chocolate in a parchment cone (see page 25), snip a small opening in the cone's tip, and pipe random zigzags all over the tops of the cake balls. Place the melted white chocolate in another parchment cone and pipe zigzags all over the tops of the cake balls. Place the reserved dark chocolate in another parchment cone and finish off with zigzags of that chocolate. While the chocolate is still wet, sprinkle some miniature morsels on top of each cake ball. Refrigerate until the chocolate is set. Place each cake ball in a paper cup, if desired. Place in a single layer in an airtight container and refrigerate for up to 4 days. Bring to room temperature before serving.

Note: I like to use dark brown fluted paper cups for these, to accentuate the chocolaty nature of the cake balls.

Rum

CAKE BALLS

I love a good rum cake, the kind that is so moist and boozy that it is practically falling apart due to its liquor soaking. It was a challenge to turn this concept into a cake ball, because of course I wanted to pack in the rum flavor, but I still had to be able to roll the mixture into a ball. I pushed the rum quantity as far as I could go while still providing you with a ball shape. These cake balls must be frozen before coating; this helps them hold together. A food disher or ice cream scoop is very helpful during the ball-forming stage.

**MAKES ABOUT 52
GOLF BALL–SIZE BALLS**

1 cup sugar

¼ cup water

1 cup gold rum (see the Note)

1 batch Yellow Buttermilk Cake (page 29), baked, cooled, and crumbled

1⅔ pounds semisweet or milk chocolate, such as Callebaut, Valrhona, or Scharffen Berger, finely chopped

52 miniature fluted paper cups (optional)

1 Combine the sugar and water in a small saucepan and stir to combine. Bring to a boil over medium-high heat, swirling the pan once or twice to encourage the sugar to dissolve. Boil for 30 seconds to 1 minute, or until the sugar is dissolved. Let cool and then stir in the rum. Transfer to a large measuring cup or other container with a spout.

2 Have the crumbled cake in a wide bowl (the more surface area, the better). Drizzle some of the rum mixture over the cake crumbs, tossing the cake as you go. Your aim is to distribute the rum as evenly as possible. Keep pouring and tossing until all of the liquid is absorbed. Now use your hands to thoroughly mix the cake and rum. Roll into golf ball–size cake balls. Freeze until firm. This can be done 1 day ahead; store in an airtight container once they are firm.

3 Line two rimmed baking sheets with parchment paper or aluminum foil. Melt the chocolate in the microwave or a double boiler. Dip the balls (straight out of the freezer) one at a time in the chocolate, encouraging any excess chocolate to drip back into the container. Place, evenly spaced, on the prepared pans. Refrigerate briefly until the chocolate is set. Trim the bottoms, if needed. Place each cake ball in a paper cup, if desired. Place in a single layer in an airtight container and refrigerate for up to 4 days. Bring to room temperature before serving.

● ● ● ● ● ● ● ● ● ●

Note: Choose your rum and chocolates carefully for the best results. Use gold rum, not white, for a more pronounced rum flavor. You can even use dark rum if you prefer. I used Zaya rum from Trinidad, a 12-year-old dark, rich, reserve estate rum. I like these dipped in the highest-quality dark chocolate, but a good milk chocolate works as well. This is not a time to scrimp on rum or chocolate quality.

Pink Raspberry
CAKE BALLS

These are very pink and very girly, perfect for a girl's birthday party or a bridal shower. White cake is combined with fresh raspberries and vanilla Confectioners' Sugar Frosting. A dip in white chocolate and freeze-dried raspberries on top complete the pretty picture. To purchase freeze-dried raspberries, check your local Whole Foods store or see Resources (page 164) for the company Just Tomatoes, Etc.! (To really girly it up, use pink Wilton Candy Melts instead of white chocolate for the outer coating.)

● ● ●

1 Combine the cake and fresh berries, using a pastry blender to break down the berries. Add 2/3 cup of the frosting. Test by compressing and tasting, and add more frosting only if needed for flavor and moisture. Roll into golf ball–size cake balls. Refrigerate until firm. This can be done 1 day ahead; store in an airtight container once they are firm.

2 Line two rimmed baking sheets with parchment paper or aluminum foil. Melt the chocolate in the microwave or a double boiler. Dip the balls one at a time in the chocolate, encouraging any excess chocolate to drip back into the container. Place, evenly spaced, on the prepared pans. Sprinkle a bit of the crushed freeze-dried raspberries on top of each cake ball while the chocolate is still wet. Refrigerate briefly until the chocolate is set. Trim the bottoms, if needed. Place each cake ball in a paper cup, if desired. Place in a single layer in an airtight container and refrigerate for up to 3 days. Bring to room temperature before serving.

Note: **These look very pretty with bits of crystallized roses on top too. You can find them in some specialty and gourmet stores.**

MAKES ABOUT 48 GOLF BALL–SIZE BALLS

- 1 batch White Cake (page 34), baked, cooled, and crumbled
- 3 cups fresh raspberries
- 1/2 batch Confectioners' Sugar Frosting (page 39), ready to use
- 1 2/3 pounds white chocolate, such as Callebaut or Valrhona Ivoire, finely chopped
- 1/3 cup freeze-dried raspberries, crushed
- 48 miniature fluted paper cups (optional)

Pumpkin Spice
CAKE BALLS

This is a very easy and very moist pumpkin cake. It has a pronounced pumpkin flavor and is gently spiced. It is so moist that it will hold together on its own, with no binder needed, but I prefer the additional flavor provided by a small quantity of Cream Cheese Frosting (page 40). These can be dipped in semisweet or milk chocolate or Confectioners' Sugar Glaze (page 47).

**MAKES ABOUT 45
GOLF BALL–SIZE BALLS**

2 cups all-purpose flour

1 tablespoon plus 1 teaspoon ground cinnamon

1 tablespoon ground ginger

2 teaspoons baking powder

1 teaspoon baking soda

¼ teaspoon ground cloves

¼ teaspoon salt

⅔ cup dark raisins

½ cup toasted walnut halves, finely chopped

1½ cups sugar

1 (15-ounce) can solid-pack pumpkin

¾ cup flavorless vegetable oil, such as canola or sunflower

4 large eggs, at room temperature

1   Position a rack in the middle of the oven. Preheat the oven to 350°F. Coat the inside of a 9 x 13-inch rectangular pan with nonstick cooking spray; set aside.

2   Whisk together the flour, 2 teaspoons of the cinnamon, 1 teaspoon of the ginger, the baking powder, baking soda, cloves, and salt in a large bowl. Toss in the raisins and nuts until they are coated.

3   Whisk together the sugar, pumpkin, oil, and eggs in a medium bowl until thoroughly combined.

4   Pour the wet ingredients over the dry and whisk until combined and smooth. Pour the batter into the prepared pan.

5   Bake for about 30 minutes, or until a toothpick inserted in the center shows a few moist crumbs when removed. Let cool completely in the pan on a wire rack. The cake is ready to use. Alternatively, double-wrap the pan in plastic wrap and store at room temperature for up to 1 day before proceeding.

6   To make the cake balls, crumble the cooled cake and combine with ¾ cup of the frosting. Test by compressing and tasting, and add more frosting only if needed for flavor and moisture. Roll into golf ball–size cake balls. Refrigerate until firm. This can be done 1 day ahead; store in an airtight container once they are firm.

7 Line two rimmed baking sheets with parchment paper or aluminum foil. Toss together the remaining 2 teaspoons cinnamon and 2 teaspoons ginger. Melt the chocolate in the microwave or a double boiler. Dip the balls one at a time in the chocolate, encouraging any excess chocolate to drip back into the container. Place, evenly spaced, on the prepared pans. Sprinkle a bit of the mixed spices on top of each cake ball while the chocolate is still wet. Refrigerate briefly until the chocolate is set. Trim the bottoms, if needed. Place each cake ball in a paper cup, if desired. Place in a single layer in an airtight container and refrigerate for up to 4 days. Bring to room temperature before serving.

½ batch Cream Cheese Frosting (page 40), ready to use

1½ pounds semisweet chocolate, such as Callebaut or Ghirardelli, or milk chocolate, such as Callebaut, Ghirardelli, or Valrhona Jivara

45 miniature fluted paper cups (optional)

Red, White, and Blue

CAKE BALLS

Independence Day brings out the thematic baker in me. These cake balls are red, white, and blue inside and out. The frozen berries used with the White Cake batter are easily found in most supermarket freezer sections. Look for packages that combine blueberries, raspberries, blackberries, and sometimes strawberries, too. They can be used straight from the freezer in this recipe. The exterior of these cake balls can be decorated in a variety of ways, but I like using red, white, and blue Wilton Candy Melts and seasonal sugar decorations. Look for color-coordinated fluted paper cups as well. For the photo, we used Wilton Silver Stars edible glitter and small red and blue sugar stars from N.Y. Cake & Baking Distributor (see Resources, page 165).

**MAKES ABOUT 52
GOLF BALL–SIZE BALLS**

1 batch White Cake
(page 34), made with 1½
cups frozen mixed berries
blended into the batter
before baking

½ batch Confectioners'
Sugar Frosting (page 39),
ready to use

8 ounces red Wilton Candy
Melts

8 ounces white Wilton
Candy Melts

8 ounces blue Wilton
Candy Melts

Holiday themed or
appropriate decorations

52 miniature fluted paper
cups (optional)

1 Crumble the cooled cake and combine with ⅔ cup of the frosting. Test by compressing and tasting, and add more frosting only if needed for flavor and moisture. Roll into golf ball–size cake balls. Refrigerate until firm. This can be done 1 day ahead; store in an airtight container once they are firm.

2 Line two rimmed baking sheets with parchment paper or aluminum foil. Melt the Candy Melts separately in the microwave or double boilers. Dip the balls one at a time (about 17 of the balls in each color), encouraging any excess chocolate to drip back into the container. Place, evenly spaced, on the prepared pans. Sprinkle some of the sugar decorations on top of each cake ball while the coating is still wet. Refrigerate briefly until the coating is set. Trim the bottoms, if needed. Place each cake ball in a paper cup, if desired. Place in a single layer in an airtight container and refrigerate for up to 3 days. Bring to room temperature before serving.

Note: **Because of the fruit you are mixing into the cake batter, the baking time for the cake might be slightly longer than in the White Cake recipe.**

Red Velvet

CAKE BALLS

Red velvet cake has a very light cocoa flavor, which is wonderful with cream cheese frosting. Use your choice of coating—these work nicely with dark, milk, or white chocolate.

● ● ●

**MAKES ABOUT 42
GOLF BALL–SIZE BALLS**

1 batch Red Velvet Cake (page 33), baked, cooled, and crumbled

½ batch Cream Cheese Frosting (page 40), ready to use

1⅓ pounds semisweet, milk, or white chocolate, such as Callebaut or Ghirardelli, finely chopped

Red colored sugar or glitter

42 miniature fluted paper cups (optional)

1 Combine the cake and about ¾ cup of the frosting. Test by compressing and tasting, and add more frosting only if needed for flavor and moisture. Roll into golf ball–size cake balls. Refrigerate until firm. This can be done 1 day ahead; store in an airtight container once they are firm.

2 Line two rimmed baking sheets with parchment paper or aluminum foil. Melt the chocolate in the microwave or a double boiler. Dip the balls one at a time in the chocolate, encouraging any excess chocolate to drip back into the container. Place, evenly spaced, on the prepared pans. Sprinkle a bit of red sugar or glitter on top of each cake ball while the chocolate is still wet. Refrigerate briefly until the chocolate is set. Trim the bottoms, if needed. Place each cake ball in a paper cup, if desired. Place in a single layer in an airtight container and refrigerate for up to 3 days. Bring to room temperature before serving.

Rocky Road
CAKE BALLS

Chocolate, marshmallows, and nuts. Start with the Fudgy Brownie recipe and simply add the suggested quantity of whatever nuts you like during the batter preparation (the original candy bar was made with cashews, but feel free to use whatever nut you like). Also, note that the marshmallows are used in three ways: mixed into the batter, added after baking, and as decoration. The ones baked into the brownie melt somewhat and add a chewy marshmallow texture that enhances the unique quality of this cake ball. These are dense and rich—for those with a major sweet tooth.

1 Crumble the cooled brownie and combine with 1 cup of the marshmallows. You will have to be firm and use your hands for the best results. You might find a squeezing action is needed with this hefty cake ball in order to form it into rounds. Roll into golf ball–size cake balls. Refrigerate briefly while you melt the chocolate and prepare the pan. This can be done 1 day ahead; store in an airtight container.

2 Line a rimmed baking sheet with parchment paper or aluminum foil. Chop the remaining ¼ cup of marshmallows and set aside with the ¼ cup of nuts; these will be for decoration. Melt the chocolate in the microwave or a double boiler. Dip the balls one at a time in the chocolate, encouraging any excess chocolate to drip back into the container. Place, evenly spaced, on the prepared pans. Sprinkle a few marshmallow pieces and nuts on top of each cake ball while the chocolate is still wet. Refrigerate briefly until the chocolate is set. Trim the bottoms, if needed. Place each cake ball in a paper cup, if desired. Place in a single layer in an airtight container and refrigerate for up to 4 days. Bring to room temperature before serving.

Note: This cake ball is made with a dense brownie, while the S'mores recipe on page 131 is made with a lighter chocolate cake. Feel free to mix and match the base for either cake ball.

**MAKES ABOUT 23
GOLF BALL–SIZE BALLS**

1 batch Fudgy Brownies (page 37), made with ½ cup nuts and ½ cup miniature marshmallows

1¼ cups miniature marshmallows

¼ cup chopped nuts (of the same type you used inside the brownie)

1 pound semisweet chocolate, such as Callebaut or Ghirardelli, finely chopped

23 miniature fluted paper cups (optional)

S'mores

CAKE BALLS

S'mores are usually made over an open fire with roasted marshmallows. This recipe does take some license with the concept by skipping the roasting step. I suggest combining chocolate cake, chocolate ganache, mini marshmallows, and crushed graham crackers for a version you can whip up in your home kitchen.

1 Combine the cake with 3 cups of the marshmallows, 2½ cups of the graham cracker crumbs, and 1¼ cups of the ganache. You might have to work a bit to get these ingredients to come together. Test by compressing and tasting, and add more ganache if needed for flavor and moisture. Roll into golf ball–size cake balls. Refrigerate until firm. This can be done 1 day ahead; store in an airtight container once they are firm.

2 Line two rimmed baking sheets with parchment paper or aluminum foil. Chop the remaining 1 cup of marshmallows and set aside with the remaining ½ cup of graham cracker crumbs; these will be for decoration. Melt the chocolate in the microwave or a double boiler. Dip the balls one at a time in the chocolate, encouraging any excess chocolate to drip back into the container. Place, evenly spaced, on the prepared pans. Sprinkle a few marshmallow pieces and graham cracker crumbs on top of each cake ball while the chocolate is still wet. Refrigerate briefly until the chocolate is set. Trim the bottoms, if needed. Place each cake ball in a paper cup, if desired. Place in a single layer in an airtight container and refrigerate for up to 4 days. Bring to room temperature before serving.

Note: Crush the graham crackers by hand until most of the pieces are between ¼ inch and ½ inch in size. There will be some fine crumbs, but try to keep some of the pieces a bit larger, as described, so that they hold up within the cake ball. Also, feel free to mix and match the base for this cake ball with the denser brownie base of the Rocky Road recipe on page 129.

MAKES ABOUT 70 GOLF BALL–SIZE BALLS

1 batch Super-Easy Chocolate Cake (page 31), baked, cooled, and crumbled

4 cups miniature marshmallows

3 cups coarsely crumbled graham crackers

1 batch Dark Chocolate Ganache (page 42), at room temperature, ready to use (should be soft and spreadable)

2⅛ pounds semisweet chocolate, such as Callebaut or Ghirardelli, finely chopped

70 miniature fluted paper cups (optional)

Toffee–Brown Butter–Pecan
CAKE BALLS

This recipe starts with a buttered pecan toffee made on top of the stove, which can be prepared several days ahead. A version of confectioners' sugar frosting made with browned butter further accentuates the toasty, nutty flavors in this cake ball. Of all the white chocolate–covered cake balls in the book, this one appeals most to even milk and dark chocolate lovers. I think the nuts temper the white chocolate's sweetness, as does the browned butter flavor.

MAKES ABOUT 70 GOLF BALL–SIZE BALLS

PECAN TOFFEE:

4 tablespoons (½ stick) unsalted butter, cut into pieces

½ cup sugar

Pinch of salt

¾ cup toasted pecan halves

FROSTING:

6 tablespoons (¾ stick) unsalted butter, at room temperature

3 cups sifted confectioners' sugar

2 tablespoons whole milk

1 teaspoon pure vanilla extract

1 To make the pecan toffee: Line a rimmed baking sheet with parchment paper or aluminum foil and spray with nonstick cooking spray. Melt the butter in a wide sauté pan, then stir in the sugar until coated (it will look grainy). Add the salt and pecans and cook over medium heat, stirring often, until the sugar liquefies and caramelizes and coats the nuts, and the caramel turns a dark toasty brown, about 3 minutes. Immediately scrape out onto the prepared pan and let cool completely. The toffee may be transferred to an airtight container and stored at room temperature for up to 3 days. When ready to use, transfer large chunks of toffee to the bowl of a food processor fitted with the metal blade and process until finely ground (you need 1 cup for the cake balls, plus a bit more for sprinkling on top).

2 To make the frosting: Place 4 tablespoons of the butter in a small saucepan and cook over medium heat until melted and browned, but not burned. It should turn a dark golden brown color. Let cool. In a medium bowl with an electric mixer on medium-high speed, beat the browned butter, the remaining 2 tablespoons butter, the sugar, milk, and vanilla until creamy, about 2 minutes, scraping down the bowl once or twice.

recipe continues

1 batch Yellow Buttermilk
Cake (page 29), baked,
cooled, and crumbled

2⅛ pounds white
chocolate, such as
Callebaut or Valrhona
Ivoire, finely chopped

70 miniature fluted paper
cups (optional)

3 Combine the cake with 1 cup of the ground pecan toffee and 1¼ cups of the frosting. Test by compressing and tasting, and add more frosting only if needed for flavor and moisture. Roll into golf ball–size cake balls. Refrigerate until firm. This can be done 1 day ahead; store in an airtight container once they are firm.

4 Line two rimmed baking sheets with parchment paper or aluminum foil. Melt the chocolate in the microwave or a double boiler. Dip the balls one at a time in the chocolate, encouraging any excess chocolate to drip back into the container. Place, evenly spaced, on the prepared pans. Sprinkle a bit of ground toffee on top of each cake ball while the chocolate is still wet. Refrigerate briefly until the chocolate is set. Trim the bottoms, if needed. Place each cake ball in a paper cup, if desired. Place in a single layer in an airtight container and refrigerate for up to 4 days. Bring to room temperature before serving.

Valentine's Day

CAKE BALLS

Red velvet cake has become the darling of the millennium and, thanks to its red hue, is perfect for a St. Valentine's Day cake ball. Enhanced with Cream Cheese Frosting and dipped in an array of white chocolate and red and pink chocolate coatings and then further embellished with decorations, these are a hit at parties and bake sales—and they make a great gift for a special loved one. Be sure to take advantage of all the colorful fluted paper cups made especially for this holiday.

● ● ●

1 Combine the cake and about ¾ cup of the frosting. Test by compressing and tasting, and add more frosting only if needed for flavor and moisture. Roll into golf ball–size cake balls. Refrigerate until firm. This can be done 1 day ahead; store in an airtight container once they are firm.

2 Line two rimmed baking sheets with parchment paper or aluminum foil. Melt the chocolates and the Candy Melts separately in the microwave or double boilers. Dip the balls one at a time (about 14 in each color), encouraging any excess chocolate to drip back into the container. Place, evenly spaced, on the prepared pans. Sprinkle some of the decorations on top of each cake ball while the chocolate is still wet. Refrigerate briefly until the chocolate is set. Trim the bottoms, if needed. Place each cake ball in a paper cup, if desired. Place in a single layer in an airtight container and refrigerate for up to 3 days. Bring to room temperature before serving.

Note: I find that it is handy to have Valentine's cake balls for kids as well as for adults, so I often use a kid-friendly approach as well as an elegant, adult design when decorating. For this cake ball, try Wilton Fill Your Heart Sprinkles for the kids and elegant candied rose petals for the adults. Both of these can be found at specialty and gourmet stores.

**MAKES ABOUT 42
GOLF BALL–SIZE BALLS**

1 batch Red Velvet Cake (page 33), baked, cooled, and crumbled

½ batch Cream Cheese Frosting (page 40), ready to use

8 ounces semisweet chocolate, such as Callebaut, Ghirardelli, or Valrhona, finely chopped

8 ounces white chocolate, such as Callebaut or Valrhona Ivoire, finely chopped

8 ounces pink or red chocolate coating, such as Wilton Candy Melts

Holiday themed or appropriate decorations (see the Note)

42 miniature fluted paper cups (optional)

Vanilla Bean

CAKE BALLS

There are those who like dark chocolate, and then there are vanilla fans—and they are legion. This cake ball is for you, combining a white cake with a vanilla frosting that is further bolstered with two whole vanilla beans. Split them in half lengthwise and use a butter knife to scrape the moist interior (where the tiny seeds are) into the frosting.

**MAKES ABOUT 52
GOLF BALL–SIZE BALLS**

2 moist, flexible vanilla beans

1 batch Confectioners' Sugar Frosting (page 39), ready to use

1 teaspoon pure vanilla extract (optional)

1 batch White Cake (page 34), baked, cooled, and crumbled

1¾ pounds white chocolate, such as Callebaut or Valrhona Ivoire, finely chopped

52 miniature fluted paper cups (optional)

1 Scrape the inside of the vanilla beans into the frosting and beat well to combine. Add the vanilla extract, if desired (there is already some in the frosting recipe). Combine the cake and ¾ cup of the frosting. Test by compressing and tasting, and add more frosting only if needed for flavor and moisture. Roll into golf ball–size cake balls. Refrigerate until firm. This can be done 1 day ahead; store in an airtight container once they are firm.

2 Line two rimmed baking sheets with parchment paper or aluminum foil. Melt the chocolate in the microwave or a double boiler. Remove and reserve ¼ cup of the melted chocolate. Dip the balls one at a time in the larger amount of chocolate, encouraging any excess chocolate to drip back into the container. Place, evenly spaced, on prepared pans. Refrigerate briefly until the chocolate is set.

3 Place the reserved melted chocolate in a parchment cone (see page 25), snip a small opening from the tip, and pipe a design of your choice on top of each ball. Refrigerate again until the chocolate is set. Trim the bottoms, if needed. Place each cake ball in a paper cup, if desired. Place in a single layer in an airtight container and refrigerate for up to 3 days. Bring to room temperature before serving.

Note: **The white-on-white look of these cake balls is very pretty in its austerity. If you want to fancy them up, pipe a neat spiral with the extra white chocolate, as suggested. Once chilled and firm, add a few drops of vodka or almond extract to ½ teaspoon of edible silver powder and blend until you reach a paint-like consistency. Use a small artist's brush to paint the spirals silver for a very upscale look. See Resources (page 164) for silver powder.**

Vegan Chocolate

CAKE BALLS

The Super-Easy Chocolate Cake combined with 100 percent fruit spread (a non-sugar-sweetened jam) and dipped in a vegan-friendly dark chocolate makes the perfect vegan cake ball. Make sure to use chocolate made with soy lecithin—or no lecithin at all—and, of course, no dairy products. Ghirardelli and Callebaut semisweet chocolates are vegan and perfect for this recipe. These cake balls are so moist that they are the perfect candidate for a dry coating, such as shaved chocolate. I have presented the recipe to you with half the batch dipped in melted chocolate and half rolled in chocolate shavings—two looks in one recipe with no extra ingredients.

1   Combine the cake and about 1 cup of the fruit spread. Test by compressing, and add as much of the remaining fruit spread as the cake will hold. Roll into golf ball–size cake balls. Refrigerate until firm. This can be done 1 day ahead; store in an airtight container once they are firm.

2   Line two rimmed baking sheets with parchment paper or aluminum foil. Melt the chopped chocolate in the microwave or a double boiler. Dip half of the balls one at a time in the chocolate, encouraging any excess chocolate to drip back into the container. Place, evenly spaced, on the prepared pans. Refrigerate briefly until the chocolate is set. Trim the bottoms, if needed. Use a chef's knife to shave small shards off of the block of chocolate. Roll the remaining balls in the chocolate shavings. Place each cake ball in a paper cup, if desired. Place in a single layer in an airtight container and refrigerate for up to 3 days. (The ones dipped in chocolate will most likely keep for an additional day.) Bring to room temperature before serving.

**MAKES ABOUT 60
GOLF BALL–SIZE BALLS**

1 batch Super-Easy
   Chocolate Cake
   (page 31), baked, cooled,
   and crumbled

1¼ cups 100% fruit
   spread, such as raspberry,
   strawberry, or apricot

1 pound semisweet
   chocolate, such as
   Callebaut or Ghirardelli,
   finely chopped

1 (1-pound) block semisweet
   chocolate, such as
   Callebaut or Ghirardelli

60 miniature fluted paper
   cups (optional)

Zesty Lemon

CAKE BALLS

When I eat a lemon dessert, I want it to be as puckery as possible. This is one of those cake balls for which you want to add as much binder as possible, in this case lemon curd, to add flavor. These are very moist and very lemony. They might keep for a day or two longer than the instructions suggest, but the brightness of the lemon flavor will diminish.

● ● ●

MAKES ABOUT 68 GOLF BALL-SIZE BALLS

1 batch Yellow Buttermilk Cake (page 29), made with 1 tablespoon freshly grated lemon zest added with the vanilla extract

1 batch Lemon Curd (page 45), ready to use

2⅛ pounds white chocolate, such as Callebaut or Valrhona Ivoire, finely chopped

⅓ cup candied lemon peel, finely minced

68 miniature fluted paper cups (optional)

1   Crumble the cooled cake and combine with 1½ cups of the lemon curd. Test by compressing, and add as much of the remaining lemon curd as the cake will hold. Roll into golf ball–size cake balls. Refrigerate until firm. This can be done 1 day ahead; store in an airtight container once they are firm.

2   Line two rimmed baking sheets with parchment paper or aluminum foil. Melt the chocolate in the microwave or a double boiler. Dip the balls one at a time in the chocolate, encouraging any excess chocolate to drip back into the container. Place, evenly spaced, on the prepared pans. Place a bit of candied peel on top of each cake ball while the chocolate is still wet. Refrigerate briefly until the chocolate is set. Trim the bottoms, if needed. Place each cake ball in a paper cup, if desired. Place in a single layer in an airtight container and refrigerate for up to 3 days. Bring to room temperature before serving.

4

Cake Ball Creations

This chapter presents fun and interesting desserts to make with your cake balls, ranging from cake ball "pops" to an ice cream cake. The idea is to get you thinking about how cake balls can be used in creative ways. Beyond what I have presented, how about little cake ball snowmen, with different size cake balls stacked on top of one another? Or a string of cake balls assembled on a platter to resemble a necklace or a caterpillar? Let your imagination soar. Send photos of your creations to me at dede@dedewilson.com and I will post them on my website.

Teddy Bears

Who doesn't like a teddy bear? These bear-iffic cake balls are perfect for a little boy's birthday party or a baby shower. The cake balls are covered in fondant and then facial details can be painted with melted chocolate or food coloring pens. The look of the bears can be tailored to your color/flavor scheme or preference—perhaps baby blue, white for a polar bear look, or even black and white for a panda. You can tint white fondant to your color of choice, or you can buy tinted or flavored fondant made by Wilton (see Resources, page 166). You can choose whatever cake balls you like for the interior of your bears, but it is best to stick with a basic cake and frosting, as opposed to something elaborate like the crème brûlée cake balls. The amount of fondant recommended is generous, but you need extra to roll out rounds with which to cover the cake balls. Once the fondant is formed around the cake balls, you'll have to remove the excess; such is the nature of cake decorating with fondant. For the photo, we used Wilton's Chocolate Rolled Fondant and then painted the eyes, nose, and smile with a black food coloring pen.

1 Have the two sizes of cake balls rolled, chilled, and ready to use.

2 If you are not using white or tinted fondant, the first step is to color your fondant. Use a toothpick to add dots of food coloring to the white fondant and knead well until the color is evenly blended. For darker colors, wear foodservice gloves or other rubber gloves to protect your fingers and hands from becoming stained.

3 Roll out a small piece of fondant to a circle 6 inches in diameter and about 1/32 inch thick. Place a cake ball on top of the circle and gather the fondant up and around the cake ball, smoothing with your fingers and palms. Gather the fondant together on top of the cake ball and pinch and twist it so that it completely encloses the ball. You might find it easier to pick up the cake ball and perform this smoothing and cover-ing technique off of the work surface. Pinch off any extra fondant and make the closure spot as smooth as possible, but don't worry, because

MAKES 20 CAKE-BALL BEARS

20 golf ball–size cake balls of choice, uncoated, chilled (for the bears' bodies)

20 slightly smaller cake balls of choice, uncoated, chilled (for the bears' heads)

About 20 toothpicks

60 ounces white fondant, such as Wilton Ready-to-Use Rolled Fondant, or colored/flavored fondant of choice

Gel food coloring in choice of color(s)

recipe continues

it will be hidden. Repeat with the remaining cake balls. Flip all of the balls over so that the seam where you closed the fondant is on the bottom of the ball. Press a toothpick into the center top of each of the larger balls so that it goes about halfway into the body. Then attach a smaller cake ball (the head) to the toothpick.

4 Make a fondant "glue" by mashing a tiny bit of fondant in a small bowl with a few drops of water until it is very sticky and soft. Set aside.

5 Make ears by rolling small balls of fondant, then flattening them slightly with your fingers to thin them out. Brush the bottoms of the ears with "glue" and attach them to the sides of the head by pressing gently. Roll out small balls for paws, press slightly into a disc shape, and use a thin, sharp paring knife to cut slits for fingers and toes. Roll out a small dome shape for the muzzle. Attach paws and muzzles with "glue" as well.

6 Use a clean brush dipped in the melted chocolate to paint eyes, nose, mouth, insides of ears, and any other embellishments you would like. Alternatively, use the edible pen to create these details. Use the photo while you are working for help and inspiration.

7 The bears are ready to serve. They may be stored at room temperature in an airtight container overnight.

Note: **If you have a lot of fondant left over and are still feeling creative, you can make extra items for the bears to hold, such as flowers or tiny toys, or you can make hats for them to wear. Be creative and make yours unique.**

2 ounces semisweet, white, or milk chocolate, melted (optional)

Small, pointed artist's brushes (if using chocolate for decoration) or Wilton FoodWriter Edible Color Marker in black (optional)

CAKE BALL
Sundae Bar

This is a party dessert for 12 or more and is somewhere between a sundae bar and a fondue party. Guests spear cake balls in varying flavors on forks or skewers, dip them in the melted chocolate of their choice, and sprinkle them with one or more of a selection of toppings. These cake balls are meant to be eaten right away, before the melted chocolate hardens. It's a bit messy, very interactive, and always a lot of fun. I have done this for kids' and adults' birthday parties alike, and it is always a hit. If you have a heating tray, use it to keep the chocolates warm and fluid while serving.

SERVES AT LEAST 12

About 50 cake balls, uncoated—consider Super-Easy Chocolate Cake (page 31) combined with Dark Chocolate Ganache (page 42); Fudgy Brownies (page 37) rolled into balls; or White Cake (page 34), Super-Easy Yellow Cake (page 30), or Yellow Buttermilk Cake (page 29) combined with Confectioners' Sugar Frosting (page 39)

1 cup toasted chopped nuts, such as walnuts, pecans, or peanuts

1 cup sweetened long-shred coconut

1 cup miniature semisweet chocolate morsels

1   Make sure the cake balls are well chilled. They should be cold so that they stay on the skewers or forks when pierced.

2   Place toppings—nuts, coconut, morsels, toffee bits, and sprinkles—in individual bowls and set on the buffet table. Place skewers or forks in a tall glass and place on the buffet table, too, along with small plates and lots of napkins.

3   Shortly before serving, melt the chocolates separately in microwaveable bowls or in double boilers. (If you use attractive microwaveable bowls, you can bring the melted chocolates right to the buffet table and also rewarm them easily, if necessary.) While the chocolates are melting, arrange the cake balls in separate large, wide bowls or piled attractively on platters and set on the table. Preheat a warming tray, if you have one, and set the melted chocolates on it. Alternatively, you might have to rewarm the chocolates if the party goes on for an extended period of time.

4 Invite guests to spear a cake ball, dip it in their chocolate of choice, place on their plate, and sprinkle one or more toppings on top of their cake balls. Guests can fill their plates with 3 or 4 cake balls for an array of flavor combinations.

Note: If you own or can borrow fondue pots, they are also ideal for keeping the melted chocolates warm during serving.

1 cup toffee bits, such as Skor or Heath

1 cup rainbow sprinkles

1 pound white chocolate, such as Callebaut or Valrhona Ivoire, finely chopped

1 pound milk chocolate, such as Callebaut or Ghirardelli, finely chopped

1 pound semisweet chocolate, such as Callebaut or Ghirardelli, finely chopped

CAKE BALL

Pops

Cake balls attach quite nicely to lollipop sticks, which makes them more of a candy-like treat. I find that the best cake balls to turn into cake pops are the ones with a firmer texture. Brownie balls are perfect, but at the very least you must use a cake and binder (cake alone won't work), and any cake ball must be chilled well, which will help the lollipop stick remain inserted when you're coating the ball with chocolate. Pay close attention to the dipping technique for the best-looking cake pops; your chocolate or coating must be very fluid in order for your cake pops to have the neatest appearance. Refer to page 24 for information on thinning your coatings, if necessary. You will also need a piece of Styrofoam to perch the cake pops in as they dry. I use a 12-inch Styrofoam cake dummy purchased at a cake-decorating supply store, but you can use any large, thick piece of Styrofoam.

● ● ●

MAKES 24 CAKE POPS

12 x 3-inch (round or square) Styrofoam cake dummy

12 ounces chocolate or coating of your choice, finely chopped

24 lollipop sticks (6-inch sticks work well)

24 golf ball–size cake balls, uncoated (your choice of cake and binder), chilled

Assorted sprinkles and sugar decorations (optional)

24 (3 x 4-inch) clear plastic bags, such as Wilton Clear Treat Bags

Ribbon

1   Line two rimmed baking sheets with parchment paper or aluminum foil. Wrap the Styrofoam with aluminum foil (to keep it clean for reuse).

2   Melt the chocolate in the microwave or a double boiler. The cake balls will have a slightly flattened area from being stored; this is where you will insert the lollipop stick. One at a time, dip the end of a lollipop stick about ¼ inch deep into the melted chocolate, then insert the stick about halfway into the ball through the flattened area. A small dot of chocolate will probably form at the juncture where the stick meets the cake. Holding the end of the stick, insert the ball into the melted chocolate, submerging the cake ball until the chocolate just comes up and over the dot of chocolate at the stick-ball juncture. Twirl the pop in place so that the cake is completely covered. (Do not drag it around the bowl, as the pull of the chocolate might dislodge the stick.) Remove from the melted chocolate and let any excess chocolate drip back into the container. This might take a few moments, so do not rush this step. Having finished cake balls that look neat and perfectly round largely depends on this step. You can tap the stick very gently against the edge of the container to encourage more chocolate to drip away. (Do not

tap too vigorously, though, or the cake ball will detach from the stick.) Once there is no extra chocolate dripping from the cake pop, insert the free end of the lollipop stick into the Styrofoam. (If you try to press it in slowly, it might not go through the foil easily; you need to use a quick stabbing motion to get the job done. Alternatively, you can make holes with a sharp metal skewer first, then insert the lollipop sticks). Repeat until all the cake balls are dipped. If you want to decorate your pops with sprinkles or sugar decorations, apply them while the chocolate is still wet. Refrigerate the cake pops until the chocolate is set.

3   Place each pop into a treat bag, stick pointing up, and seal shut by tying a ribbon right underneath the pop. Place gently in an airtight container and refrigerate for up to 3 days. Bring to room temperature before serving.

Note: Lollipop sticks come in various lengths. I find the 6-inch ones to be easiest to handle. The lollipop sticks and clear treat bags can be found at craft stores and through mail-order (see Resources, page 164).

Fairy Princess Ballerinas

Okay, as an adult I know that fairies are very hard to find, princesses are rare, and being a ballerina is hard work. But little girls like to dress up like all of them, and sometimes they like to mix and match their metaphors. These are girly cake balls, which can be gussied up to be any of these frilly, fancy characters or a combo of all three—FPBs, if you will. It is best to make these cake balls (which form the lower part of the FPBs) with a basic cake and frosting. The decorating makes a great birthday party activity. Have the balls dipped in chocolate and chilled and the rest can be done en masse with your real-life FPBs. The very sparkly edible glitter on the FPB's skirt shown in the photo is called Disco Dust. It comes in many colors and can be found through Beryl's (see Resources, page 164).

● ● ●

MAKES 20 FAIRY PRINCESS BALLERINAS (FPB) CAKE BALLS

20 cake balls of choice, rolled slightly larger than golf balls, uncoated, chilled

1 pound white chocolate, such as Callebaut or Valrhona Ivoire, finely chopped

55 ounces white fondant, such as Wilton Ready-to-Use Rolled Fondant

About 20 thin bamboo skewers (7 to 12 inches long; found in most supermarkets)

Gel food coloring in choice of colors

Granulated sugar, white or colored

1 Have the cake balls rolled, chilled, and ready to use.

2 Line two rimmed baking sheets with parchment paper or aluminum foil. Melt the white chocolate in the microwave or a double boiler. Dip the balls one at a time in the chocolate, encouraging any excess chocolate to drip back into the container. Place, evenly spaced, on the prepared pans. Refrigerate briefly until the chocolate is set. Trim the bottoms, if needed. Place in a single layer in an airtight container and refrigerate for up to 2 days. Bring to room temperature before proceeding.

3 Tint 15 ounces of fondant to whatever color you would like the FPBs' skin tone(s) to be. Tint another 15 ounces of fondant to whatever color you would like the upper bodices to be. For both of these batches, use a toothpick to add dots of food coloring color to the white fondant and knead well until the color is evenly blended. For darker colors, wear foodservice gloves or other rubber gloves to protect your fingers and hands from becoming stained. Roll the bodices into gently squared-off rounds slightly smaller than the cake balls. Roll the skin-tinted fondant into round heads proportionately smaller than the bodices. Roll thin ropes of the remaining skin-tinted fondant for arms and hands. Use the photo for help and inspiration.

recipe continues

Round cookie cutters in various sizes between 2½ inches and 3¼ inches

2 ounces semisweet, white, or milk chocolate, melted (optional)

Small, pointed artist's brushes (if using chocolate for decoration)

Wilton FoodWriter Edible Color Marker in any colors desired (optional)

Wilton Icing Writer in any colors desired (optional)

Tiny candies and sugar decorations for embellishment, such as sugar pearls, dragées, or sprinkles of various colors and shapes

4 Take a quarter of whatever fondant is left, wrap it well in plastic wrap, and set aside. If desired, tint the remaining fondant as described above to whatever color you would like for the skirts. Sprinkle your work surface with edible glitter in a color that complements the skirt color. Roll out this fondant a little at a time to a ⅟₃₂-inch thickness on top of the glitter, then cut out circles of various diameters between 2½ and 3¼ inches to make various length skirts. Take a cake ball, drape a skirt circle on top, and press gently to make the skirt adhere and to help it drape attractively around the ball. Depending on the size of the circle you cut, you might have the look of a full-length skirt or a shorter one.

5 Once your cake balls, fondant bodices, and fondant heads are formed, line them up on their sides on your work surface and measure the total length of a grouping. Cut bamboo skewers about 1 inch shorter than this total length. Press a skewer into the center top of the cake ball so that it goes about halfway into the ball, then attach the fondant bodice and fondant head. Trim the skewer if needed so that it is completely encased within the FPB. Repeat with the remaining FPBs.

6 Make a fondant "glue" by mashing a tiny bit of fondant in a small bowl with a few drops of water until it is very sticky and soft. Attach arms to the sides of the FPBs using a bit of "glue" applied with a brush to the end of the arms. Press to help adhere.

7 The remaining reserved fondant can be used to make hair and accessories. (The hair is a must! Accessories are optional.) Tint as desired. Press through a clean garlic press to make long hair and arrange on the heads as you like. Alternatively, roll out very thin and cut out pieces to make blunt bangs, side-swept bangs, a bob, or another style of your choice. Again, use the photo for help and inspiration.

8 Any remaining fondant can be tinted and made into wands, crowns, flowers for the hair, tiaras, pocketbooks, or even wings. With a paring knife, food coloring, and imagination, the sky is the limit. Attach any fondant accessories with "glue."

9 Eyes, noses, and mouths can be painted, using a pointed brush, with melted chocolate, or you can use the FoodWriter pens. The pens or the Icing Writers can be used to embellish the dresses and accessories or any part of your FPBs. You can also use the Icing Writers to make tiny dabs of frosting where you can, if you like, affix a candy or sugar decoration.

10 The FPBs are ready to serve. They may be stored at room temperature in an airtight container for up to 6 hours.

Note: **If the edible glitter does not adhere well to the fondant while rolling it out, don't fret. When you finish making your FPBs, use beaten raw egg white (or reconstituted egg white powder) as glue. Brush it onto the skirts with a small brush, then sprinkle edible glitter on top or use another dry brush to apply.**

Easter Egg
CAKE BALLS

Cake balls can easily be formed into oval shapes to make a seasonal dessert for Easter. I have chosen pastel colors as decoration, but feel free to decorate as you like. I recommend a simple white cake and vanilla icing, but again, feel free to alter the cake and binder. The Zesty Lemon Cake Balls (page 138) work wonderfully as well. Just make sure your outer coating is white chocolate—the better to show off the colored decorations. I have presented you with three different types of decoration. Read the recipe through first to decide whether you would like to use all three or choose one or two that you particularly like.

●　●　●

MAKES ABOUT 45 EGG-SIZE "BALLS"

1 batch White Cake (page 34), baked, cooled, and crumbled

1 batch Confectioners' Sugar Frosting (page 39), ready to use

2 pounds white chocolate, such as Callebaut or Valrhona Ivoire, finely chopped

Assorted colored sugars and edible glitter

Edible gold, silver, or colored powders

Vodka or almond extract

Small artist's brushes

45 standard-size fluted paper cups (optional)

1　Combine the cake and about 1 cup of the frosting. Test by compressing and tasting, and add more frosting only if needed for flavor and moisture. Roll into egg-size ovals. Refrigerate until firm. This can be done 1 day ahead; store in an airtight container once they are firm.

2　Line two rimmed baking sheets with parchment paper or aluminum foil. Melt the chocolate in the microwave or a double boiler. Remove and reserve ¼ cup of the melted chocolate. Dip the ovals one at a time in the larger amount of chocolate, encouraging any excess chocolate to drip back into the container. Place, evenly spaced, on the prepared pans. Sprinkle colored sugar or glitter on top of half of the egg balls while the chocolate is still wet, covering the tops and sides as completely as possible. You might need to use a spoon to scoop up the sugar or glitter and apply to the sides of the eggs. Refrigerate all the eggs briefly until the chocolate is set.

3　For the egg balls that are still unadorned, I recommend two different approaches. For the first approach, place the reserved melted chocolate in a parchment cone (see page 25), snip a small opening from the tip, and pipe a design of your choice on top of half of the remaining eggs. Chill briefly again to firm the piping.

4 Now mix up your "paints," placing about ½ teaspoon of the gold, silver, or colored powders in small individual bowls. Add only enough vodka or almond extract to reach a paint-like consistency. Using a brush, paint free-form designs on the remaining unadorned eggs. You may also apply paint to the raised decorations made by the piped chocolate on the others, if desired. The paint will dry almost immediately. Trim the bottoms of all the eggs, if needed. Place each egg ball in a paper cup, if desired. Place in a single layer in an airtight container and refrigerate for up to 3 days. Bring to room temperature before serving.

Note: **You can also melt different colors of Wilton Candy Melts and use those to pipe decorations onto the dipped eggs.**

CAKE BALL

Pumpkins

These are ideal for Halloween, Thanksgiving, or any fall birthday party or special occasion. The diminutive pumpkins have really tasty cake balls inside. While you could tint fondant green and brown to make the stems, I have taken a cue from my talented food stylist friend, Karen Tack, and her partner, stylist, and photographer extraordinaire, Alan Richardson. (Check out their book *Hello, Cupcake!* [Houghton Mifflin, 2008] for all sorts of fun baking ideas.) They hit the candy aisle for ideas and recommend making pumpkin stems from green licorice twists and using candy fruit snacks for the tendrils. You can choose your favorite cake and frosting flavors for the interior, but why not go with the Pumpkin Spice Cake Balls on page 124? There will be extra fondant left over, from which you can make mini pumpkins to go alongside. In fact, an array of various sizes of pumpkins makes a great-looking pumpkin patch.

MAKES 20 PUMPKIN-SHAPED CAKE BALLS

20 cake balls of choice, rolled to about 2½ inches in diameter, uncoated, chilled

60 ounces orange fondant, such as Wilton Ready-to-Use Rolled Fondant

Orange gel food coloring (optional)

Twizzlers Rainbow Twists (you will use the green portion) or Twizzlers Chocolate Twists (these are brown)

1 Have the cake balls rolled, chilled, and ready to use.

2 You can use the orange fondant as is, or make it an even richer color by adding orange food coloring. In the latter case, use a toothpick to add dots of color to the fondant and knead well until the color is evenly blended. Wear foodservice gloves or other rubber gloves to protect your fingers and hands from becoming stained.

3 Roll out a small piece of fondant to a circle 8 inches in diameter and about 1/32 inch thick. Place a cake ball on top of the circle and gather the fondant up and around the cake ball, smoothing with your fingers and palms. Gather the fondant together on top of the cake ball and pinch and twist it so that it completely encloses the ball. You might find it easier to pick up the cake ball and perform this smoothing and cover-ing technique off of the work surface. Pinch off any extra fondant and make the closure spot as smooth as possible, but don't worry, because

it will be hidden. Repeat with the remaining cake balls. Flip all of the balls over so that the seam where you closed the fondant is on the bottom of the ball.

4 Press down the center top of the pumpkins gently to help create a pumpkin shape. You want to have a depression right on top and the sides bulging out a bit. Use the back of a butter knife to make vertical ridges around each pumpkin. If you like, you can paint stripes of orange coloring down inside the "stripes" to accentuate them.

5 Cut short pieces of the green or brown Twizzlers and insert these pieces as stems. Peel apart the Streamers to separate the green ropes from the rest. Cut these ropes into various lengths, twist them around a pencil, slip them off, and arrange on top of the pumpkins as tendrils, inserting one end near the stem.

6 The pumpkins are ready to serve. They may be stored overnight at room temperature in an airtight container.

Kellogg's Fruit Streamers Watermelon Madness fruit snacks (you will use the green portion)

Small, pointed artist's brush (optional)

Cake Ball Christmas

Sometimes the whole is more than the sum of its parts, as in this case where individual cake balls are assembled on a platter in a Christmas tree shape. This is very easy to make and the final look and size is completely up to you; just as we all have distinctive decorations for our real Christmas trees, so can we uniquely decorate this one. Get the kids involved—even preschoolers can affix decorations with frosting. You can pipe garlands with frosting as we did for the photo, but you could also use licorice laces or a different candy or confectionery approach. The "ornaments" can be anything from silver and gold *dragées* to small, round cinnamon candies or sugar stars, all of which are affixed with a dot of icing. For the photo, we used gold *dragées*, red and clear sugar "jewels," and yellow-tinted frosting ornaments. For our topper we used clear sugar stars and painted them with edible gold powder. You will need a very large flat platter or tray. The size will depend on how large you make your "tree." You can also cover a large, thick piece of cardboard with aluminum foil, or with colored foil from a floral or craft store. Make sure that all of your balls are the same size for the best result.

MAKES 1 LARGE CHRISTMAS TREE

- 20 to 25 golf ball–size cake balls of choice, uncoated, chilled
- 1¼ pounds green confectionery coating, finely chopped
- 3 ounces semisweet chocolate, such as Ghirardelli or Callebaut, finely chopped
- ½ batch Confectioner's Sugar Frosting (page 39), ready to use

1 Have the cake balls rolled, chilled, and ready to use.

2 Line two rimmed baking sheet pans with parchment paper or aluminum foil; set aside. Melt both the confectionery coating and the chocolate, separately, in the microwave or a double boiler. Dip 4 of the cake balls, one at a time, in the semisweet chocolate, encouraging any excess chocolate to drip back into the container. Place, evenly spaced, on the prepared pans. Dip the remaining balls one at a time in the green coating, encouraging any excess coating to drip back into the container. Place, evenly spaced, on the prepared pans. Refrigerate briefly until the chocolate is set. Trim the bottoms, if needed. Place in a single layer in an airtight container and refrigerate for up to 2 days. Bring to room temperature before proceeding.

recipe continues

- Gel food coloring in choice of colors (optional)
- Pastry bag and coupler
- Decorating tips, such as a small star tip (Wilton #18 or similar) and a #2 plain round tip
- Wilton Sparkle Gel (optional; great for "lights")
- Tiny candies and sugar decorations for embellishment, such as sugar pearls, *dragées*, or sprinkles of various colors and shapes
- White edible glitter, such as Wilton Cake Sparkles (optional)

3 Follow these steps to create the Christmas tree shape: Place one green cake ball in the center top of the platter. Place two or three below it, making the second row. The number of every subsequent row will depend on the size of your balls and how they fit together; all the balls should be close and touching and extend on either side of the previous row. Continue to make rows with the green-coated balls, each row slightly wider than the last. The final row should be slightly narrower and have fewer balls than the one above. Use the photo for help and inspiration. Arrange the 4 semisweet chocolate–covered balls at center bottom, in two rows of two, to create the "trunk."

4 If desired, tint about 1 cup of the frosting with food coloring for garlands. Use the pastry bag, coupler, and star tip to pipe garlands, or use another decorative tip you like to create the look you want. Follow the photo for ideas. Use the Sparkle Gel to pipe shapes to mimic lights, if you like, or other shapes. Use additional frosting as "glue" for sugar decorations and *dragées*. Tint additional frosting as desired to pipe Christmas "balls" or other decorations. Sprinkle edible glitter over all for a sparkly effect. All of these decorating ideas are up to you. It's your tree! Decorate to your heart's content.

5 Your Christmas tree is ready to serve. It may be stored at room temperature for up to 6 hours.

Note: The tree "topper" can be anything you want. For example, you could "glue" a star-shaped cookie to the top of the tree or wrap the top cake ball in gold or silver foil.

The Cake Ball Tower

This is my cake ball homage to the classic French *croquembouche*. That dessert is composed of a tower of filled cream puffs stuck together with melted caramelized sugar. Here I have "glued" cake balls together with additional melted chocolate for a grand showstopper of a dessert. It's great for buffet parties. You can use any cake balls that you like, although I do think this looks best if all the balls are dipped in the same color chocolate. The melted chocolate "glue" can also be used to affix decorations, such as *dragées* or molded sugar decorations, to the tower. You can use golf ball–size balls, or for a more delicate look, use smaller cake balls. Make some room in your refrigerator to let the finished tower firm up before serving.

1 Melt the chocolate in a microwave or double boiler. Place some of the melted chocolate in a parchment cone (see page 25) and snip a small opening from the tip.

2 Arrange a circle of cake balls on a platter, creating a ring about 10 inches in diameter. The cake balls should be touching one another. Completely fill the center of the ring with more cake balls, all touching one another. From above, looking down, pipe a bit of chocolate from the parchment cone at every juncture where the cake balls touch, which will be approximately halfway down their sides.

3 Create another slightly smaller layer of cake balls in a similar manner on top of the first layer, again "gluing" the points of contact with the melted chocolate. Keep repeating layers until you have formed a cone-shaped tower of cake balls. You can add additional cake balls here and there to fill in gaps, if necessary. Use a more generous amount of melted chocolate in these instances to make sure they stick to the tower. Use additional melted chocolate to affix decorations, as desired. Refrigerate the tower until the "glue" is firm. To serve, guests pick off cake balls as they like.

Note: When you start trying to serve the cake balls, know that some come off easily, while others break apart. Don't worry! This never keeps anyone from enjoying this charming, towering treat.

SERVES AT LEAST 12

8 ounces chocolate (whatever was used to coat cake balls)

About 50 golf ball–size cake balls, 75 walnut-size balls, or 100 1-inch balls, dipped and chilled until firm

***Dragées* or other decorations, as desired**

12-inch flat platter

The Ice Cream

CAKE BALL CAKE

This recipe is fun to make and to look at and can be customized using your favorite flavors. All you need is a 9 x 3-inch springform pan and your imagination. Quite simply, it is ice cream formed into a traditional round cake shape with uncoated cake balls embedded inside the ice cream. A coating of ganache tops the cake. When you cut wedges of the frozen treat, you will see polka dots made from the cake balls! This visual impact is best if the cake and ice cream are contrasting colors. I have provided you with the required amounts of each, no matter what flavors you choose. It is important to use a premium ice cream such as Häagen-Dazs, as it freezes to a hard texture, which helps create a neater-looking cake.

● ● ●

**MAKE ONE 9-INCH CAKE;
SERVES 12**

1 gallon premium ice cream

30 golf ball–size cake balls, uncoated, frozen

8 ounces chocolate of your choice, finely chopped

2 cups ganache of your choice

1 Soften the ice cream for a few minutes, just until it is fairly easy to scoop. Scoop a scant half of the ice cream into a 9-inch round spring-form pan and use the back of a large, strong spoon to press it down to make as level a layer as possible. Place 18 of the cake balls, evenly spaced, on top of the ice cream. Press some of them down firmly into the ice cream, press others down just a little bit, and leave the rest on the surface of the ice cream so that they are all on slightly different levels in a random pattern.

2 Scoop more ice cream on top of the balls and use a small spoon to make sure that you fill all the spaces between the balls with ice cream. Keep adding ice cream and pressing it down until the ice cream is about ¼ inch below the top of the pan. (You might not use all of the ice cream.) Use a small offset spatula to smooth the top of the ice cream to make it level. Place in the freezer to firm up for at least 6 hours or up to overnight.

3 Line a rimmed baking sheet with parchment paper or aluminum foil. Melt the chocolate in the microwave or a double boiler. Dip the remaining balls one at a time in the chocolate, encouraging any excess chocolate to drip back into the container. Place, evenly spaced, on the

prepared pan. Refrigerate briefly until the chocolate is set. Trim the bottoms, if needed.

4   At least 3 hours before serving, melt the ganache in the microwave or on the stovetop. Let cool until it is just warm—not hot but still fluid. Working quickly, pour ganache all over the surface of the frozen ice cream cake and tilt the cake back and forth and side to side to encourage the ganache to flow over the top of the cake, entirely covering the surface. Use an offset spatula to help the process, if necessary. Freeze again until the ganache is solid.

5   Right before serving, unmold the cake from the pan and arrange the dipped cake balls evenly along the outer top edge of the cake. Serve immediately, cutting into wedges so that a dipped ball is centered on the edge of each piece.

Note: There are so many combinations you could try in this cake. Just for starters, there's pumpkin ice cream and Gingerbread Cake Balls (made with Cream Cheese Frosting) with Milk Chocolate Ganache on top; mint chocolate chip ice cream and plain chocolate cake balls (made with Dark Chocolate Ganache) with semisweet chocolate ganache on top; and vanilla ice cream and Chocolate Chip Cookie Dough Cake Balls with Dark Chocolate Ganache on top.

Raspberry Hearts

While these are an obvious choice for Valentine's Day, they are also perfect for any day you want to say "I love you" with a sweet treat. Chocolate cake, fresh raspberries, and dark chocolate ganache are combined and pressed into a baking pan. Once frozen, the mixture is cut out into heart shapes, which are then dunked in chocolate. Edible gold powder, either brushed on dry or painted on wet, is a lovely finishing touch.

● ● ●

MAKES ABOUT 22 2-INCH HEARTS

1 batch Super-Easy Chocolate Cake (page 31), baked, cooled, and crumbled

3 cups fresh raspberries

½ batch Dark Chocolate Ganache (page 42), made with Valrhona Manjari or Scharffen Berger semisweet, at room temperature, ready to use (should be soft and spreadable)

2-inch heart-shaped biscuit cutter (see the Note)

2 pounds dark chocolate, such as Valrhona Guanaja or Manjari or Scharffen Berger semisweet, finely chopped

1 Line a 9 x 13-inch rectangular pan with plastic wrap so that it is overhanging on all sides. Combine the cake and berries, using a pastry blender to break down the berries. Add 1 cup of the ganache. Test by compressing and tasting, and add more ganache only if needed for flavor and moisture. Press into an even layer in the prepared pan. Freeze until firm, at least 6 hours. This can be done 1 day ahead.

2 Remove the pan from the freezer to allow the cake mixture to soften slightly. Line two rimmed baking sheets with parchment paper or aluminum foil and set a wire rack on each one. Pull the cake up and out of the pan, using the plastic wrap to help. Remove the plastic wrap and place the chilled cake on a work surface. Use the biscuit cutter to cut out as many hearts as possible. (You will have scraps left over from between the hearts. Save them in a container in the freezer and fold them into vanilla or chocolate ice cream—or just snack on them!)

3 Melt the chocolate in the microwave or a double boiler. Dip the hearts one at a time in the chocolate, encouraging any excess chocolate to drip back into the container. Place, evenly spaced, on the prepared racks. Refrigerate briefly until the chocolate is set. Place about 1/2 teaspoon of the gold powder in a small bowl. Add only enough vodka or almond extract to reach a paint-like consistency. Using the brush, paint free-form designs on the hearts. The paint will dry almost immediately. Run a knife around the base of the hearts so that they come up off of the rack neatly. Place each heart in a paper cup, if desired. Place in a single layer in an airtight container and refrigerate for up to 3 days. Bring to room temperature before serving.

Note: Biscuit cutters are extra deep, which makes forming these hearts much easier than when using the more typically shallow cookie cutters. The cutters you use should be about 1 1/2 inches deep. Also, a cooling rack with a crisscross pattern of bars will support your hearts better than a rack with only parallel bars.

Edible gold powder
Vodka or almond extract
Small artist's brush
22 standard-size fluted paper cups (optional)

Resources

Beryl's Cake Decorating and Pastry Supplies

P.O. Box 1584
North Springfield, VA 22151
(800) 488-2749
(703) 256-6951
Fax (703) 750-3779
www.beryls.com

There is a Beryl, and she will often answer the phone herself. Look here for high-quality baking pans, food colors, gold and silver powders, sugar decorations, fluted paper wrappers, laser-cut wrappers, cocoa butter, blocks of caramel, cake dummies, books, and more. Peruse this voluminous website for all your decorating needs.

Boyajian Incorporated

144 Will Drive
Canton, MA 02021
(800) 965-0665
(781) 828-9966
Fax (781) 828-9922
www.boyajianinc.com

This company is dedicated to flavorings and flavored oils. I love their peppermint flavor, which is used in the After-Dinner Chocolate-Mint Cake Balls (page 49) and the Peppermint–White Chocolate Cake Balls (page 98).

Chocosphere

(877) 992-4626
Fax (877) 912-4626
www.chocosphere.com

If you are looking for high-quality couverture chocolate or gianduja, order from this fabulous mail-order company. They specialize in all my favorite chocolates that are great to eat and to use in your baked goods. Owners Joanne and Jerry Kryszek offer excellent personal service, and they ship nationwide.

J&D Foods

(866) 692-3980
www.baconsalt.com

This company makes bacon salt (which is, surprisingly, vegetarian and kosher!) as well as a host of other bacon-related items. See the Milk Chocolate Bacon Bourbon Cake Balls on page 106, which use bacon salt as an optional topping.

Just Tomatoes, Etc.!

P.O. Box 807
Westley, CA 95387
(800) 537-1985
(209) 894-5371
Fax (209) 894-3146
www.justtomatoes.com

This company makes freeze-dried fruits and vegetables that are crisp and colorful and have very true flavor. The fruits, including raspberries, bananas, blackberries, cherries, and blueberries, add color and flavor to cake balls, especially as decoration. You can order them direct or look for them in specialty stores and Whole Foods stores. Look for the dried raspberries in the Chocolate-Raspberry Cake Balls (page 72) and the Pink Raspberry Cake Balls (page 123).

King Arthur Flour

P.O. Box 876
Norwich, VT 05055
(800) 827-6836
(802) 649-3881
Fax (800) 343-3002
www.kingarthurflour.com

This catalog and website offers high-quality flours, extracts, chocolates, scales, measuring cups (including handy ones in odd sizes), Zeroll food scoops, and more. You can find bulk caramel here in smaller amounts, such as an 18-ounce size.

Kitchen Krafts, Inc.

P.O. Box 442
Waukon, IA 52172
(800) 298-5389
(800) 776-0575
(563) 535-8000
Fax (800) 850-3093
www.kitchenkrafts.com

This company has a fabulous selection of fluted paper wrappers, laser-cut wrappers, baking pans, chocolate, chocolate coatings, Paramount Crystals, lollipop sticks, and decorating supplies of all sorts. Shop here for peanut butter–flavored coatings and all the Guittard flavored/colored coatings: orange-colored orange flavor, pink-colored strawberry flavor, yellow-colored lemon flavor, and green-colored mint flavor.

LorAnn Oils

4518 Aurelius Road
Lansing, MI 48909
(517) 882-0215
(888) 456-7266
Fax (517) 882-0507
www.lorannoils.com

This company specializes in high-quality oils of all flavors that can be added to confectionery coating. Try the Creamy Hazelnut or Irish Crème in a milk chocolate coating or the Strawberry-Banana in a pink-colored coating.

N.Y. Cake & Baking Distributor

56 West 22nd Street
New York, NY 10010
(212) 675-2253
(800) 942-2539
Fax (212) 675-7099
www.nycake.com

This New York institution offers a variety of high-quality chocolates, food colors, gold and silver powders, pastry bags and decorating tips, baking pans, parchment paper, cake dummies, lollipop sticks, clear treat bags, and many *dragées* and sugar decorations. They also have a large selection of mini fluted paper wrappers.

Sugarcraft

3665 Dixie Highway
Hamilton, OH 45015
(513) 896-7089
www.sugarcraft.com

Look here for all kinds of sugar decorations, fluted paper wrappers, food colors, gold powder, Paramount Crystals, and many different choices for chocolate, chocolate coatings, and more. They carry Merckens coatings as well as all the

Guittard flavored/colored coatings: orange-colored orange flavor, pink-colored strawberry flavor, yellow-colored lemon flavor, and green-colored mint flavor. They also have white-colored yogurt-flavored coating. This company has the molded sugar carrots used on page 63. They stock white lollipop sticks as well as plastic ones in brilliant colors.

Sur La Table

P.O. Box 840
Brownsburg, IN 46112
(800) 243-0852
Fax (317) 858-5521
www.surlatable.com

This fabulous mail-order company also has stores throughout the country. They have a great selection of KitchenAid mixers, baking pans, silicone spatulas, measuring implements, mixing bowls, chocolate, cocoa powder, chocolate dipping tools, lovely serving pieces, and much more.

Williams-Sonoma

3250 Van Ness Avenue
San Francisco, CA 94109
(877) 812-6235
Fax (702) 363-2541
www.williams-sonoma.com

This well-known company offers quality baking pans, tools, some ingredients, KitchenAid mixers, measuring implements, and more.

Wilton Industries, Inc.

2240 West 75th Street
Woodridge, IL 60517
(630) 963-1818
(800) 794-5866
Fax (630) 963-7196
www.wilton.com

This great catalog offers heavy-duty pans, food colors, parchment paper, Candy Melts, white and colored fondant, fluted paper wrappers, sugar decorations, lollipop sticks, clear treat bags, edible glitter in star and heart shapes, storage solutions, and much more. You can often find Wilton items at Michaels crafts stores.

Zeroll Products

P.O. Box 999
Fort Pierce, FL 34954
(800) USA-5000
www.zeroll.com

This company makes the best ice cream scoops, which just happen to portion out cake balls perfectly. They call them Universal EZ Dishers on the site, and they come in many sizes. I use the #40 for my standard-size cake balls.

Measurement Equivalents

Please note that all conversions are approximate.

Liquid Conversions

U.S.	Metric
1 tsp	5 ml
1 tbs	15 ml
2 tbs	30 ml
3 tbs	45 ml
¼ cup	60 ml
⅓ cup	75 ml
⅓ cup + 1 tbs	90 ml
⅓ cup + 2 tbs	100 ml
½ cup	120 ml
⅔ cup	150 ml
¾ cup	180 ml
¾ cup + 2 tbs	200 ml
1 cup	240 ml
1 cup + 2 tbs	275 ml
1¼ cups	300 ml
1⅓ cups	325 ml
1½ cups	350 ml
1¾ cups	375 ml
1¾ cups	400 ml
1¾ cups + 2 tbs	450 ml
2 cups (1 pint)	475 ml
2½ cups	600 ml
3 cups	720 ml
4 cups (1 quart)	945 ml
	(1,000 ml is 1 liter)

Weight Conversions

U.S./U.K.	Metric
½ oz	14 g
1 oz	28 g
1½ oz	43 g
2 oz	57 g
2½ oz	71 g
3 oz	85 g
3½ oz	100 g
4 oz	113 g
5 oz	142 g
6 oz	170 g
7 oz	200 g
8 oz	227 g
9 oz	255 g
10 oz	284 g
11 oz	312 g
12 oz	340 g
13 oz	368 g
14 oz	400 g
15 oz	425 g
1 lb	454 g

Oven Temperature Conversions

°F	Gas Mark	°C
250	½	120
275	1	140
300	2	150
325	3	165
350	4	180
375	5	190
400	6	200
425	7	220
450	8	230
475	9	240
500	10	260
550	Broil	290

Index

Note: Page references in *italics* indicate photographs.

y

z

About the Author

Dede Wilson has written over a dozen cookbooks, including *Unforgettable Desserts*, *Truffles*, *The Birthday Cake Book*, *Wedding Cakes You Can Make*, *The Wedding Cake Book* (which was nominated for an IACP Julia Child Award), and the popular Baker's Field Guide series. She is a contributing editor at *Bon Appétit* and a frequent guest on the *Today* show, *The Early Show*, and HSN. Dede has hosted two cooking series on public television and has appeared on CNN, the Food Network, HGTV, and the Discovery Channel. She lives in Amherst, Massachusetts. Come visit her at dedewilson.com.